CLASSIC WARPLANES

SUPERMARINE SPITFIRE

Mike Spick

a Salamander book

Published by Salamander Books Limited
LONDON • NEW YORK

A SALAMANDER BOOK

Published by
Salamander Books Ltd.,
129–137 York Way,
London N7 9LG,
United Kingdom.

© Salamander Books Ltd. 1990

ISBN 0–86101–535–5

Distributed in the United Kingdom by
Hodder & Stoughton Services, PO Box 6,
Mill Road, Dunton Green, Sevenoaks,
Kent TN13 2XX.

All rights reserved. No part of this book may
be reproduced, stored in a retrieval system or
transmitted in any form or by any means,
electronic, mechanical, recording or
otherwise, without the prior permission of
Salamander Books Ltd.

All correspondence concerning the content
of this volume should be addressed to the
publisher.

CREDITS

Editor: Bob Munro
Designers: Oxprint Ltd.
Colour artwork: © Pilot Press Ltd.
Three-view, side-view and cutaway drawings:
© Pilot Press Ltd.
Filmset by Oxprint Ltd., The Old Mill,
Flairplan Typesetting Ltd.
Colour reproduction by Graham Curtis Repro
Printed in Belgium by Proost International
Book Production, Turnhout.

ACKNOWLEDGEMENTS

The publishers are indebted to Bruce Robertson
for his invaluable contribution to this work.

AUTHOR

MIKE SPICK was born in London less than three weeks before the Supermarine
Spitfire made its maiden flight. Educated at Churchers College, Petersfield
(a school with a strong naval interest!), he later entered the construction industry and
carried out considerable work on RAF airfields.

An occasional broadcaster on aviation topics, Mr. Spick's interests include
wargaming, which led him to a close study of air warfare, followed by a highly
successful first book, "Air Battles in Miniature" (Patrick Stephens). Other books to
his credit include the Salamander titles, "Modern Air Combat" (with Bill Gunston),
"B-1B Fact File", F-4 Phantom II Fact File" (with Doug Richardson), "F-14 Fact
File", and "Modern Fighting Helicopters", as well as contributing to "The Battle of
Britain".

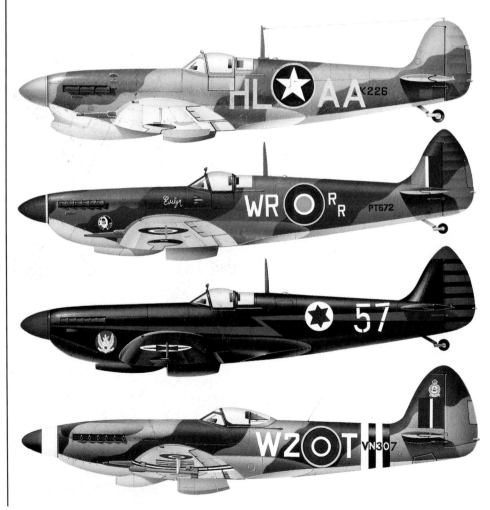

CONTENTS

DURING the early-1930s, the bomber was a slow, fabric-covered biplane, ill-armed and with its crew exposed to the elements. The only real defence against it was the fighter; also a biplane, but faster, better armed and manoeuvrable enough to take on any enemy fighters that might accompany the bombers. While not an ideal solution, the fighter was also reckoned to be fairly effective against the bombers themselves. Then almost overnight, the scenario changed. The spearhead of the revolution was the fast bomber, designed to carry the war to the military and industrial heart of an enemy country. It was a monoplane with a retractable undercarriage, carrying a heavier bomb load much farther, higher and faster than its biplane counterpart.

Then as now, fighter procurement had to be directed against a future rather than the present threat. The time taken from initial concept to squadron service was measured in years rather than months; the threat having to be evaluated and the

Above: Big, slow and cumbersome, the Handley Page Heyford typified the biplane bombers serving in the years between the wars. But a new generation was about to take over.

counter prepared well in advance. By 1935, several bombers which were capable of cruising speeds of 180mph (290 km/hr) or more, at altitudes of 20,000ft (6,100m), had either flown or were in an advanced stage of development. The standard RAF interceptor at this time was the Gloster Gauntlet, which first entered service in May of 1935. An open-cockpit biplane, the Gauntlet had a top speed of 230mph (370km/hr), and took nine minutes to reach 20,000ft (6,100m). The problems of interception are obvious: during the time the Gauntlet took to reach altitude, the bomber(s) would have travelled 27 miles (43.4km). If the fighter was not scrambled in good time, it would fail to intercept. If the bomber made even a mild change of course, it would not be where the fighter expected it to be; while

Left: Appropriately nicknamed the "Flying Pencil", Dornier's Do 17 spearheaded the new generation of sleek and swift monoplane bombers entering service during the 1930s.

Supermarine Spitfire

Above: Although its performance was credible, the Gloster Gladiator was the last biplane fighter to enter front-line RAF service.

in cloudy weather, formations of fighters and bombers could pass each other without a sighting. If it was in the right place, but just one minute late, the fighter would lag the bomber by three miles (48km). It would then take nearly four minutes to close to a firing position astern – provided that the bomber did not see it and open the throttles, in which case the fighter might never catch it. Even if the fighter managed to attack, but failed to destroy the target, it would take far too long for it to reposition for a second attempt. Under these conditions, attempts at interception by the fighters of the day were likely to be ineffective. The next generation of interceptors would need a much faster rate of climb, and a significant speed advantage. Realistically, this could only be achieved by a monoplane fighter, with a retractable undercarriage and an enclosed cockpit.

MEETING THE THREAT

The primary task of the Royal Air Force (RAF) was the defence of the British Isles; the defence of British colonies and dominions was regarded as important but secondary. The perceived threat to Britain during the 1930s was from the growing might of Germany's new Luftwaffe, and many believed that this would take the form of unescorted mass bomber raids launched from airfields in Germany. Soon, the Air Ministry was taking steps to develop a counter to the German bomber threat. In fact, a truer description would be interceptor. The main requirement was to catch a force of bombers as quickly as possible and inflict unacceptable casualties on it. Unacceptable casualties meant shooting down at least one in every eight bombers taking part in each raid. The accepted wisdom of the time was that the bomber would always get through; but the effectiveness of a bombing raid could be reduced considerably by the disruption of the formation. The defending

country simply had to soak up the damage until the cumulative effect of attrition wore away either the enemy's will or his means to continue the raids. Not for a long while was anyone to consider the possibility of France and the Low Countries being overrun, thus providing the Luftwaffe with fighter bases within striking distance of British shores, thus making escorted bomber raids a distinct possibility. On the other hand, fighter combat in the defence of British colonies and dominions was always probable, although this consideration could not be allowed to influence the primary scenario.

It is often said that the moment produces the man. In this case it produced not only the man, but the engine. Both were exactly right for the moment. The man was Reginald J. Mitchell, Chief Designer at the Supermarine Aircraft Company, a small aircraft manufacturer located near the floating bridge over the River Itchen at Southampton, England. The engine was the renowned Rolls-Royce Merlin.

Above: The man behind the machine: R.J. Mitchell's experience in the design of high-speed floatplanes was to prove crucial when it came to designing a new fighter.

History and Development

Above: The Supermarine S.5 was one of several monoplane floatplanes designed to participate in races for the Schneider Trophy. Small and very fast, these floatplanes were to prove extremely successful.

Mitchell's early reputation was founded on the design of flying boats and racing seaplanes; an unlikely mixture for a man who was to design a fighter which was to become legendary. His first venture into the fighter world was Supermarine's response to Air Ministry Specification F.7/30, issued in late 1931. This, the Supermarine Type 224, was a cranked-wing, fixed-gear design, powered by the Rolls-Royce Goshawk engine using evaporative cooling. It proved to be not particularly fast, had a poor rate of climb, and troubles with the cooling system were experienced. Of the seven F.7/30 entrants, the winner was the highly-manoeuvrable Gloster Gladiator, which entered service in 1937 as the last of the RAF's biplane fighters.

Meanwhile, a far superior engine, the PV.12, was being developed by Rolls-Royce, the company that had built the Type R engines that had powered Mitchell's record-breaking S.6B floatplanes.

Rolls-Royce decided late in 1932 to produce a new engine with a V-12 configuration as a private venture, using as much technology from the Type R as possible. The new engine would deliver at least 750hp, but be capable of development to produce at least 1,000hp. It was named Merlin, after the bird of prey rather than the Arthurian wizard. Meanwhile, Mitchell had been operated on for cancer in 1933; as part of his recuperation he had visited Germany and seen the growth in that country's military might. Convinced that the outbreak of war was only a matter of time, he drove himself to produce a superior fighter. As luck would have it, the advent of the Merlin engine coincided with Mitchell's development of the Type 224. The extra power it offered, combined with a small frontal area, was exactly what he needed.

KILLING MACHINES

Later production models of the Spitfire bore all the hallmarks of a machine built for war: strength, robustness, speed and an almost brutal impression of power. They were killing machines, and they looked the part. Not so the first prototype and the early production models. These gave an impression of grace and beauty, almost of delicacy. This is part of the Spitfire legend, and it invites comparison with two of the Spitfire's counterparts: the Hawker Hurricane, a large bully of a fighter which was its stablemate in the epic Battle of Britain, and the small, angular Messerschmitt Bf 109E, its main opponent in the same conflict. In weaponry terms, the Hurricane was a broadsword, the Bf 109 a spear, while the

Below: Photographed at Eastleigh shortly after its completion in early-1936, K5054 was the prototype Type 300 Spitfire. From the outset, it was clear that this new fighter had the look of a real winner.

Above: A portrait of a winning team, caught high in the skies above England. While a brace of Spitfires hold formation in the background, the foreground is dominated by a Hawker Hurricane.

Spitfire was a rapier, an instrument of delicacy and precision.

The prototype Spitfire as it finally emerged was a very sleek machine. The critical factors in determining the fuselage cross-section were the frontal area of the Merlin engine, and the size of the pilot to be accommodated. The engine and its accessories were laid out with upper and lower fuel tanks located just behind, and the fuselage then tapered back to the tail. The cockpit was narrow as a result, and it fitted a burly pilot like a glove. Entry was from the left, via a small drop-down door. The first Spitfires had a straight perspex one-piece sliding canopy, but this was bulged at an early stage in production to give taller pilots extra headroom. This compared favourably with the Bf 109's cockpit, which simply could not accommodate very tall pilots. By contrast, the hood of the German fighter hinged sideways, and the heavy metal framework obscured much of the pilot's vision. It was found in early models of the Spitfire that the sliding hood was extremely difficult to open at high speeds; a wholly unsatisfactory feature in a war machine which the pilot may have to abandon in a hurry. Fortunately, the problem was soon cured by means of a small knock-out panel which the pilot could break with his elbow, thus equalizing the cockpit pressure with that of the ambient air. Just behind the sliding hood was a further perspex area affording a view to the rear. Later, a rear view mirror was fitted to give the pilot a better chance of spotting an attacker coming in from astern.

Above: When fully kitted out in flying suit, and with a large parachute pack in tow, the larger pilot found the narrow cockpit to be a tight fit.

Below: Scramble! Access to the cockpit was greatly helped by the provision of an integral drop-down door in the port fuselage.

History and Development

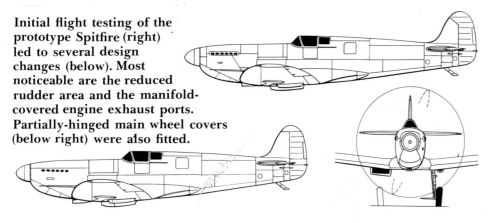

Initial flight testing of the prototype Spitfire (right) led to several design changes (below). Most noticeable are the reduced rudder area and the manifold-covered engine exhaust ports. Partially-hinged main wheel covers (below right) were also fitted.

The engine cowling of the Spitfire was almost flat across the top surface, then curving down sharply to give a mullet-headed appearance. It ran forward almost level with the bottom of the windscreen, which impeded the pilot's view considerably. This could be embarrassing, both on the ground and in the air. On the ground, successful taxying was achieved by swinging the nose from left to right and back again, in order to see what was in front; not surprisingly, collisions with various ground obstacles were to become an all too frequent occurrence. In the air, all was well until a high-deflection shot at a turning opponent was needed, when the target would vanish all too soon beneath the Spitfire's long nose. A few

outstanding marksmen overcame this handicap, but as the average pilot was not a good shot anyway, this mattered rather less than it might appear. In the Hurricane, powered by the same Merlin engine, the pilot sat up higher, which gave him a slightly better downward view over the nose; but the advantage was debatable because the raised cockpit caused additional drag, which in turn reduced the aircraft's overall performance slightly.

The first Spitfires had a two-bladed, fixed-pitch propeller. The pitch angle was a compromise, which meant that the propeller was most efficient only in the middle of the performance envelope. These units were soon changed for three-bladed, two-pitch propellers, the settings

of which were optimized for take-off and cruising. This was better, as it shortened the take-off run considerably, but it had the disadvantage that in the rapidly changing conditions of aerial combat, the engine was often either overspeeding or labouring, rather as a modern car engine would be if it could only use first and fourth gears. In 1940, a constant-speed unit was fitted to all aircraft, thus enabling the Merlin engine to perform efficiently at all altitude/speed combinations. This in turn improved both acceleration and rate of climb, as well as raising the Spitfire's service ceiling by an appreciable amount.

The tailoring of the Merlin into a streamlined carapace of the lowest possible frontal area, while necessary to obtain the utmost performance from the available power, meant that the engine accessories had to be shoehorned in wherever they would go. Consequently, both the coolant header tank and the oil reservoir were located in front of the engine. If either were hit, the Merlin would quickly overheat and seize up. A fixed-gun fighter

Below: Early-production Spitfires sported a two-bladed, fixed-pitch propeller, but successful tests were soon being conducted with three-bladed, two-pitch units.

Above: At best, the fit of the Rolls-Royce Merlin powerplant into the Spitfire's engine casing could be described as "snug".

must point directly at a target in order to shoot at it, thus making the forward fuselage the biggest target for any return fire (from the gunners of a bomber, perhaps), and therefore the most likely area to be hit. The location of these tanks made them, and thus the Spitfire, very vulnerable, although in all fairness it is difficult to see where else they could have been reasonably located where protection would have been greater.

FUEL TANKS

Another area of vulnerability was in the positioning of the fuel tanks immediately in front of the cockpit, although these were partly shielded by the engine and were self-sealing against small-calibre perforations. This again was a compromise, as fuel tanks have to be grouped around or on the aircraft's centre of gravity (c.g.) if trim is not to be seriously upset as the fuel is consumed. Also, several hundreds of pounds of fuel slopping around in half-empty tanks can upset the handling of the aircraft during manoeuvring flight, unless they are correctly positioned.

The most striking feature of the Spitfire was its beautiful wing shape, which has

often been described as being elliptical. This is not quite true. The leading-edge was a sort of flattened half ellipse, a feature which arose from the need to use a single main spar; while the trailing-edge was far more obviously elliptical in shape.

The elliptical wing has often been described as aerodynamically perfect, and the shape does give the lowest induced drag for a given amount of lift. However, like everything else in fighter design, the definitive wing shape of the Spitfire arose from a compromise between conflicting requirements. A fighter wing has to have a good lift/drag ratio; that is to say, it must supply adequate lift without producing a high penalty in drag. It needs a moderate aspect ratio, resulting in a compromise between turning and rolling ability: a high aspect ratio confers a small turn radius but slow roll rate, while a low aspect ratio allows a high roll rate but causes a high level of drag in a hard turn. The wing has to be strong enough to resist the heavy loadings imposed in manoeuvring flight, and stiff enough to resist the torsional forces arising from the same cause. At the same time, it must not be too heavy structurally, and it should be deep enough to contain all required equipment. Ideally, it should be relatively easy to

manufacture. The Spitfire wing met all of these conditions, with the possible exception of the ease of manufacture.

Perhaps the single most important feature of the Spitfire's wing was the correct choice of thickness/chord ratio. Using the National Advisory Committee for Aeronautics (NACA) 2200 series aerofoil section, the ratio was 13 per cent at the root, decreasing to six per cent at the tip. This was remarkably thin for the period, and was one of the main reasons for the ability of the Spitfire to be developed through many successive variants, each getting faster and faster. The thin wing resulted in minimal profile drag, as well as keeping the critical Mach number relatively high. Air moving past a curved surface has to travel faster to cover the increased distance, and with a fighter diving at high speed it can soon reach the transonic zone in which buffeting occurs. The thin wing of the Spitfire delayed the onset of buffeting to speeds far beyond the reach of most of its contemporaries.

Below: Camouflaged in dark earth and dark green, this view of the prototype Spitfire illustrates the unusual (often described as elliptical) wing planform.

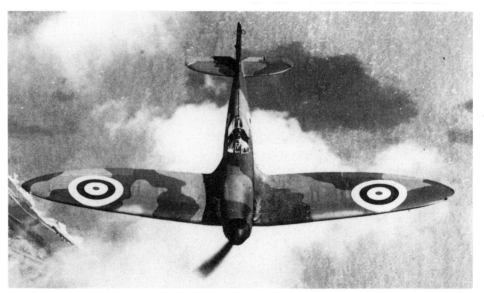

History and Development

Above: Receiving attention between sorties, this Spitfire IA carries the initial operational armament configuration of four .303in Colt Browning machine guns per wing.

The wing of the Spitfire was originally to house four .303 Colt Browning machine-guns, plus ammunition boxes holding 300 rounds per gun. This was later increased to six, and finally, before the first prototype was constructed, to eight. The wing also had to house the main undercarriage units, with the result that the main wheel hydraulic leg attachments were located close in to the wing roots, retracting outwards and upwards into wheel wells located in the underside of the wing. Four of the machine-guns were positioned outboard of each wheel well; but as they occupied almost the full depth of the wing, their ammunition boxes had to be spaced laterally. As a result, the two outboard machine-guns were positioned a long way out from the wing root.

WING DEPTH

Had the straight-taper planform been adopted, the wing would have had to have been much thicker, because a straight-taper wing starts getting thinner from the moment that it leaves the root if the

Right: Spent shell casings and belt links fall to the ground as this Spitfire IA lets rip at the butts during gun-firing checks.

Above: Easily identified by the large tail number, this Spitfire I was assigned to No.19 Squadron in late-1938. Based at RAF Duxford, Cambridgeshire, this was the first operational RAF Spitfire squadron.

Above: Several nations ordered the Spitfire in the late-1930s, but the re-equipment of RAF Fighter Command units took priority. This Spitfire I was the sole example supplied to the French Air Force before the war.

thickness/chord ratio is to remain near constant. The elliptical wing planform has the advantage because the chord remains near constant for a goodly portion of the span, until the point where the curve of the trailing-edge starts to tighten its radius towards the tip. Sufficient depth of wing is thus available over a considerable proportion of the span. On the Spitfire, the outermost guns

Above: The Spitfire's main landing gear wheeltrack was very narrow, making operations from aircraft carrier decks extremely hazardous.

were squeezed in with just the merest hint of a bulge, unnoticeable without close inspection.

Another design weakness had crept in here, as the track of the main wheels was very narrow. This did not matter too much on a peacetime airfield with a smooth concrete runway, but it did lead to problems with heavy landings by hamfisted pilots. This problem was to be aggravated when development of the Spitfire resulted in the inevitable weight increases; matters were not helped when pilots were forced to operate from bombdamaged runways or "agricultural" airfields, and it became positively critical when the Spitfire went to sea in its navalized versions. In this respect, the Spitfire was inferior to its sturdy Hawker stablemate which had a wide track main gear, although its German rival, the Bf 109E, was equally weak on its "pins".

The Spitfire's radiator was located under the starboard wing, outboard of the wheel leg junction and just behind the wheel well. Previously, radiators had been excessively draggy items which, in his quest for the highest possible speeds, R. J. Mitchell had tried hard to avoid. He had used evaporative cooling on his racing seaplanes and Type 224, but this proved unsuitable for fighter aircraft, and the problem of cooling the engine while incurring an acceptable penalty in drag remained. The solution to the problem came from the Royal Aircraft Establishment (RAE) at Farnborough. They had developed a radiator which, like later jet engine intakes, had a duct with a convergent cross-sectional area, widening from front to rear, which reduced the velocity of the airflow. As the air passed through the radiator matrix, it was heated and expanded, then given increased velocity by a divergent outlet before being expelled. In this manner a small thrust increment was gained, and while this was never enough to entirely offset the drag of the radiator, it reduced it to what was considered an acceptable level.

FLAP DESIGN

One of the great successes of the Spitfire's wing was the flap design. At an early stage it was thought that the flap area might prove to be on the high side, and that a reduction might be called for. The design was left in its original form on the premise that further development would inevitably increase the weight of the Spitfire, and that at some future date larger flaps might be needed. In fact, the Spitfire was to undergo many transformations over the following years, but while the loaded weight of the aircraft nearly doubled, the flaps remained the same size throughout the Spitfire's career.

Not quite so successful were the ailerons. The Spitfire may have been noted for its delightful handling in the medium- and low-speed ranges, but the ailerons stiffened at high speed, becoming almost immovable near terminal velocity. A fighter needs to be manoeuvrable if it is to be effective; to change direction it must use the rolling plane. In a high-speed dive, the Spitfire's roll rate became very slow because the ailerons were covered in fabric, and at very high speeds the low pressure over the upper surface caused the fabric to balloon out, deforming the aileron's shape. When combat clearly demonstrated what a handicap this was, a move was made to fit metal ailerons to all aircraft, but this modification programme was not completed until late-1941.

The Spitfire was stable both laterally and longitudinally, which made it a good gun platform. In a high-speed dive it was exceptionally stable, thanks to its low wing thickness/chord ratio. It was also a simple and easy aircraft to fly, being very responsive to the controls, especially in pitch and yaw, and it could turn tightly while being flown to its limits. Its stall characteristics were very forgiving – a critical factor in aerial combat – unlike those of the Bf 109, which was a brute. It was also a remarkably strong aircraft, being designed to take combat loadings of up to nine g.

Below: A pre-war formation of No.19 Sqn, RAF, Spitfire Is. Aircraft such as these would soon be duelling with Luftwaffe Messerschmitt Bf 109s.

THE development of the Spitfire is the story of a continuous search for ever greater performance, driven by the urgency of war. As the saying goes, "combat is the ultimate (and the unkindest) judge". The pace of technological progress during the Second World War was so fast that when one fighter established superiority over another, its reign might last no more than a few weeks before the tables were turned. During the first two years of the war, the Spitfire quickly proved that it could out-turn its principal opponent, the Bf 109E, although perhaps not by quite

Above: Almost as famous as the aircraft itself, the Rolls-Royce Merlin engine lay at the heart of the Spitfire's success story.

such a wide margin as is commonly supposed. But to the age-old question, "which was the best fighter", there can be only one answer. Superior performance, in terms of maximum speed, acceleration, rate of climb and combat ceiling (the altitude at which the rate of climb drops to 500ft/min [152.5m/min]), allows its possessor to both join and break combat at will. The best fighter is the one which can force its opponent to fight at a disadvantage. Performance is conferred by power, and the search for ever more power was to dominate the development of the Spitfire.

The Rolls-Royce Merlin engine underwent a continual process of "tweaking" to extract ever more power, while specific variants of it were developed which performed best at either very high or medium to low altitudes. In certain cases, the airframe was also modified to meet the needs of specific roles. But there are limits to what can be achieved from one basic engine, and Rolls-Royce produced a new

and much more powerful motor which powered many of the later marks of Spitfire, and which was, for various reasons, to cause fairly radical airframe modifications. With a capacity of 8 Imp gals (36.69 litres) compared to the Merlin's 6 Imp gals (26.99 litres), the new engine, named Griffon, utilized a similar V12 layout only slightly larger in frontal area than the Merlin that it succeeded, but rather heavier. While the Griffon engine gave a useful performance increment, it was never to totally outperform the Merlin. This was because its maximum rating was achieved at 2,750rpm, rather than the 3,000rpm of the smaller unit.

Other lines of development followed were to improve the Spitfire's aerodynamic efficiency; to increase the fuel capacity, without which the Spitfire would have

Above: A trio of early-production Spitfire Is bank gracefully for the camera. Few could have foreseen just how versatile the basic design would prove to be over the years.

become increasingly short-legged as both the power and the weight grew; and to increase the armament. It was also necessary to adapt the basic design to other roles, primarily carrierborne operations and photo-reconnaissance (PR) work.

A total of 1,583 Spitfire Is were built, the first of which entered service with No.19 Squadron, RAF, at Duxford in July 1938, and it was the MkIA that was to equip most Spitfire squadrons during the Battle of Britain. Another early variant was the reconnaissance-configured PR.I (with suffixes from A to G), equipped with a vertical camera. A few cannon-armed MkIBs were also produced, but these were not considered to be a success.

Above: Equipped with vertical and/or oblique cameras, the Spitfire PR.VI Type F was optimized for long-range reconnaissance tasks. Camouflaged in PRU Blue, this machine served with No.3 Photo Recce Unit (PRU), RAF.

Above: The 40 Imp gal (182 litre) long-range fuel tank under the port wing of this Spitfire IIA gave the aircraft the range to fly escort for bombers attacking German battleships as part of Operation "Sunrise".

INTO SERVICE

The first of 920 Spitfire IIs was delivered to the RAF in August 1940. This model was externally almost identical to the MkI, but the Merlin III engine was replaced by the Merlin XII, rated at 1,175hp, and which also had cartridge starting. It also carried more armour protection than the earlier models, an extra 73lb (33kg) being shared between the pilot, the glycol header tank and the upper fuel tank. Most were machine-gun armed MkIIAs, but 170 MkIIBs carried

cannon. In 1942, a handful of Spitfire IIs were modified for the air-sea rescue mission by the addition of racks for smoke markers, while provision was made for

Below: Proudly on display at RAF Duxford in May 1939, these No.19 Squadron, RAF, MkIs display the early two-bladed propeller.

Developing the Breed

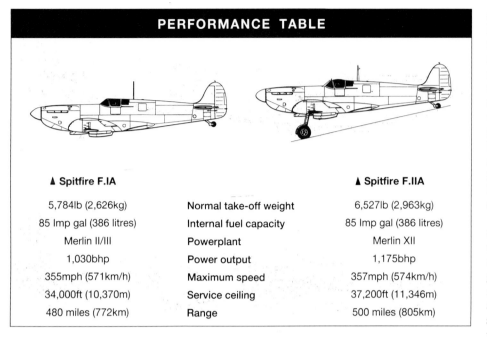

PERFORMANCE TABLE

▲ Spitfire F.IA		▲ Spitfire F.IIA
5,784lb (2,626kg)	Normal take-off weight	6,527lb (2,963kg)
85 Imp gal (386 litres)	Internal fuel capacity	85 Imp gal (386 litres)
Merlin II/III	Powerplant	Merlin XII
1,030bhp	Power output	1,175bhp
355mph (571km/h)	Maximum speed	357mph (574km/h)
34,000ft (10,370m)	Service ceiling	37,200ft (11,346m)
480 miles (772km)	Range	500 miles (805km)

dropping a dinghy and food. At first called the MkIIC, these aircraft were later redesignated ASR.II.

The next member of the Spitfire family was the MkIII, although this model was not put into full-scale production. The MkIII was to use the Merlin XX engine, which developed 1,390hp, and so the fuselage and engine mountings needed strengthening, as did the main gear legs, which were also raked forward a bit in an attempt to make the Spitfire less likely to tip onto its nose while operating in rough-field conditions. A retractable tailwheel was also incorporated. The most radical

Below: The sole High Speed Spitfire was a radically-modified MkI, but its use was limited to various research and development projects.

change was the cropping of the wing tips in an attempt to improve the aircraft's rate of roll, even at the expense of the radius of turn. This change was the first admission that getting started into the turn quickly was considered preferable to achieving the tightest radius; a factor that was to recur again later. Armament for the MkIII was to comprise four 20mm Hispano cannon, the machine-guns being deleted; but though intended as an air superiority machine *par excellence*, the Spitfire III was to be overtaken by the events of war.

Another Spitfire variant that never entered production was the MkIV. This was the first of the line to be powered by the Griffon engine, which would have given a substantial performance increment. The cowling was redesigned to accommodate the larger engine, and several structural changes made. The proposed armament comprised no less than six 20mm cannon. Wing tanks increased the overall fuel capacity to 130 Imp gals (591 litres), while larger tyres were fitted to cope with the aircraft's increased weight. Slotted flaps were also proposed, but the standard flap was found to be quite adequate. However, even before the prototype flew, the PR.IV, which was a modified MkI without armament but with extra fuel and oil capacity, and one or more cameras, entered production. The original MkIV was later redesignated the Spitfire XX.

SUPERIOR OPPONENT

While Mks III and IV were under development, the nature of the threat changed, and in January 1941, the Messerschmitt Bf 109F entered service with the Luftwaffe. Whereas the Bf 109E had been slightly superior to the Spitfire II at altitudes in excess of 20,000ft (6,100m), the Bf 109F was even better. The urgent RAF need was to counter it with a fighter capable of a higher rate of climb, greater speed, and better high altitude performance.

Above: Well over 6,000 Spitfire Vs were built, making it by far the most numerous member of the family.

Of the total production run, 3,923 were MkVBs, such as this example supplied to the USAAF.

Above: A graphic illustration of the strength built in to the wing is provided by this view of a battle-damaged Spitfire which managed to make it home after taking a hit.

Above: In contrast to the smaller Aboukir filter, this MkVC displays the prominent undernose fairing

consistent with the Vokes tropical air filter. The aircraft served in Australia during 1943.

The Spitfire III might have been the answer, but neither it nor its engine could be mass produced in the timescale that the situation demanded. The compromise answer was to install the Merlin 45 engine in a strengthened Spitfire I airframe, together with a larger radiator. This compromise solution became the Spitfire V, which was to become the most numerous of all the Spitfire variants produced. Total production was 94 MkVAs, 3,923 MkVBs, and 2,447 MkVCs.

Spitfire subtypes were by now classified by the type of wing fitted, this having been standardized into three types depending on armament. The A-wing held the original four .303in Browning machine-guns; the B-wing carried a 20mm cannon

Left: Taxying a Spitfire on the ground was never an easy procedure, primarily because the long engine cowling severely restricted the pilot's forward vision.

Developing the Breed

and two machine-guns; while the C-wing could accommodate either two cannon, one cannon and two machine-guns, or four machine-guns. There were, however, other differences between the Spitfire VA, VB, and VC. The weight of armour was increased from 129lb (58.5kg) on the MkVA to 152lb (69kg) on the MkVB and 193lb (87.6kg) on the MkVC. The MkVC also featured a strengthened main gear leg, which was set two inches (5cm) farther forward (as proposed for the MkIII), and some later aircraft had extended elevator horn balances. Many later MkVs were fitted with the Merlin 46, which gave improved performance at high altitude. The MkV was also the first variant to make extensive use of drop and overload tanks, and some models had a 29 Imp gal (131.8 litre) ferry tank in the rear fuselage. The MkV was also the first bomb-carrying Spitfire variant.

DESERT FILTER

The Spitfire V was widely used in the Middle East, and to overcome excessive engine wear caused by dust and grit ingestion, a Vokes filter was fitted beneath the nose, spoiling the clean lines and reducing performance. As there was no alternative,

Below: A variety of overload fuel tanks were fitted to Spitfire Vs to increase the fighter's operational range. Illustrated is a 90 Imp gal (410 litre) "slipper" tank.

Air Filters

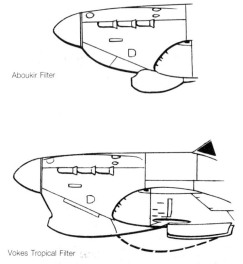

Aboukir Filter

Vokes Tropical Filter

this penalty had to be accepted. It was also in the Middle East that the need for low-altitude performance was recognized, although in Europe, a counter to German fighters making high-speed tip and run attacks at low-level was needed. This resulted in the low-altitude Spitfire LF.V, "clipped, cropped, and clapped" as the time-hallowed description runs. "Clipped" referred to the wingtips, which were shortened, as had been proposed for the MkIII. This not only improved the roll rate, albeit at the expense of turn radius, but the reduced drag improved acceleration and maximum speed. "Cropped" referred to the supercharger, the impellor of which had its radius reduced by about 0.8 inches (2cm) in

order to attain 18lb (8.1kg) of boost at 6,000ft (1,830m), and also to the altitude performance, which was considerably reduced. Boosted in this manner, the Merlin 45M engine had a relatively short life – hence "clapped".

The Spitfire HF.VI, of which only 100 were built, was a dedicated high-altitude interceptor intended to counter the pressurized Junkers Ju 86P and R which could roam England unmolested at altitudes of 40,000ft (12,200m) or more during 1940/41. This was the first Spitfire variant to make use of the extended-span wing with pointed tips, and a pressure cabin. Powered by a Merlin 47 driving a four-bladed propeller, it was just adequate for the task, but was not a great success. One fault was that the canopy was fixed in order to seal the cabin, a feature disliked by the pilots, although it could be jettisoned in an emergency.

In an effort to squeeze even more performance out of the Merlin, Rolls-Royce had developed a two-stage supercharger with aftercooler, often incorrectly called an intercooler. The result was the Merlin 60 series: longer and heavier than the previous engines, but which doubled the available horsepower at 30,000ft (9,150m), giving an unprecedented performance

Below: Banking towards the camera, this Spitfire LF.VB reveals the distinctive clipped wing tips. They bestowed greater roll rate and speed when operating at low level.

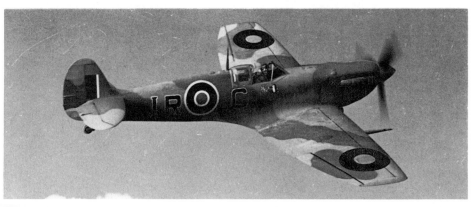

Supermarine Spitfire

Underwing Radiator Configurations

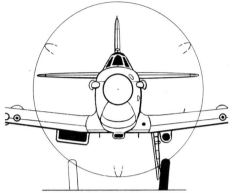

Above: This head-on view of a MkVC shows the distinctive asymmetric arrangement of the two underwing radiators. These comprised a large coolant unit (starboard) and a slimmer oil-cooler unit (port).

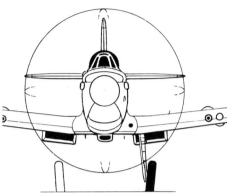

Above: Further development of the Spitfire led to changes in the underwing radiator configuration. This MkIX illustrates the switch to a pair of larger symmetrical cooling radiators.

increase at high altitudes. This gave rise to three new Spitfire variants: the Mks VII, VIII and IX.

DOUBLE RADIATOR

The Spitfire HF.VII was an extensive redesign based on the HF.VI. The extended span wing was retained, while the chord and area of the rudder were increased. The Merlin 61 needed extra cooling capacity, and one of the identifying points of this variant was that it had two radiators, one under each wing. The tail-wheel was retractable, as had been proposed for the Spitfire III. The HF.VII was slightly longer than previous Spitfires, mainly to accommodate the extra length of the engine. Service ceiling was increased to 42,500ft (12,962m), and maximum speed rose to 408mph (656km/hr). Rate of climb was vastly superior at high altitudes. A total of 140 HF.VIIs were built, these seeing considerable action in both Europe and the Middle East.

Entering service in August 1943, the Spitfire VIII combined the best of the engine and airframe advances made over the preceding years. Of the total build, 160 were extended-wing HF.VIIIs powered by the Merlin 70; 267 were F.VIIIs with the Merlin 61 or 63; while the remaining 1,231 were LF.VIIIs with Merlin 66s. C-type wings were used on the last two models, along with added fuel tanks, while many late-production aircraft featured a pointed rudder. In many ways the MkVIII was the best of the Spitfires, but as it never saw service in Northern Europe, its capabilities went largely unrecognized. There were two reasons for this: firstly, it was overtaken by events, being overshadowed by the numerically later, but operationally earlier, MkIX; secondly, the performance-reducing Vokes filter fitted to the tropical MkVC was long gone. Filters were now incorporated in the intake as standard, which made the MkVIII eminently suitable for hot climes, and they were all sent overseas. Two interesting modifications were tried on individual MkVIIIs: the first was a six-bladed, contra-rotating propeller; the second was a teardrop canopy to improve the pilot's rearward view. Both these features were adopted as standard on later production variants.

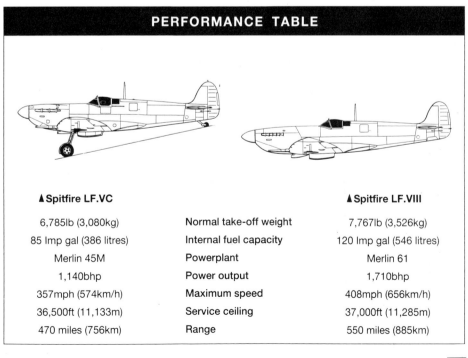

PERFORMANCE TABLE		
▲ Spitfire LF.VC		▲ Spitfire LF.VIII
6,785lb (3,080kg)	Normal take-off weight	7,767lb (3,526kg)
85 Imp gal (386 litres)	Internal fuel capacity	120 Imp gal (546 litres)
Merlin 45M	Powerplant	Merlin 61
1,140bhp	Power output	1,710bhp
357mph (574km/h)	Maximum speed	408mph (656km/h)
36,500ft (11,133m)	Service ceiling	37,000ft (11,285m)
470 miles (756km)	Range	550 miles (885km)

Developing the Breed

Supermarine Spitfire IX cutaway drawing key

1 Starboard wingtip
2 Navigation light
3 Starboard aileron
4 Browning 0·303-in (7,7-mm) machine guns
5 Machine gun ports (patched)
6 Ammunition boxes (350 rounds per gun)
7 Aileron control rod
8 Bellcrank hinge control
9 Starboard split trailing-edge flap
10 Aileron control cables
11 Cannon ammunition box (120 rounds)
12 Starboard 20-mm Hispano cannon
13 Ammunition feed drum
14 Cannon barrel
15 Rotol four-bladed constant speed propeller
16 Cannon barrel fairing
17 Spinner
18 Propeller hub pitch control mechanism
19 Armoured spinner backplate
20 Coolant system header tank
21 Coolant filler cap
22 Rolls-Royce Merlin 61 liquid-cooled Vee 12-cylinder engine
23 Exhaust stubs
24 Forward engine mounting
25 Engine bottom cowling
26 Cowling integral oil tank 5·6 Imp gal (25 l) capacity
27 Extended carburettor air intake duct
28 Engine bearer struts
29 Main engine mounting member
30 Oil filter
31 Two-stage supercharger
32 Engine bearer attachment
33 Suppressor
34 Engine accessories
35 Intercooler
36 Compressor air intake scoop
37 Hydraulic reservoir
38 Hydraulic system filter
39 Armoured firewall/fuel tank bulkhead
40 Fuel filler cap
41 Top main fuel tank, 48 Imp gal (218 l) capacity
42 Back of instrument panel
43 Compass mounting
44 Fuel tank/longeron attachment fitting
45 Bottom main fuel tank, 37 Imp gal (168 l) capacity
46 Rudder pedal bar
47 Sloping fuel tank bulkhead
48 Fuel cock control
49 Chart case
50 Trim control handwheel
51 Engine throttle and propeller controls
52 Control column handgrip
53 Radio controller
54 Bullet proof windscreen
55 Reflector gunsight
56 Pilot's rear view mirror
57 Canopy framing
58 Windscreen side panels
59 Sliding cockpit canopy cover
60 Headrest
61 Pilot's head armour
62 Safety harness
63 Pilot's seat
64 Side entry hatch
65 Back armour
66 Seat support frame
67 Pneumatic system air bottles
68 Fuselage main longeron

69 Auxiliary fuel tank, 29 Imp gal (132 l) capacity, used only in conjunction with very long range slipper tank
70 Sliding canopy rail
71 Voltage regulator
72 Cockpit aft glazing
73 IFF radio equipment
74 HF aerial mast
75 Aerial cable lead-in
76 Radio transmitter/receiver
77 Radio compartment access hatch
78 Upper identification light
79 Rear fuselage frame construction
80 Fuselage skin plating
81 Oxygen bottle
82 Signal cartridge launcher
83 IFF aerial
84 Starboard tailplane
85 Starboard elevator
86 Fin front spar (fuselage frame extension
87 Fin rib construction
88 HF aerial cable
89 Rudder mass balance
90 Rudder construction
91 Sternpost
92 Rudder trim tab
93 Trim control jack
94 Tail navigation light
95 Elevator tab

96 Port fabric covered elevator construction
97 Elevator horn balance
98 IFF aerial cable
99 Tailplane rib construction
100 Elevator hinge control
101 Rudder control rod
102 Tailplane spar/fuselage frame attachment
103 Fuselage double frame
104 Non-retracting, castoring tailwheel
105 Tailwheel strut
106 Rudder control lever
107 Sloping tail assembly joint frame
108 Tailwheel shock absorber strut

109 Battery
110 Tail control cable runs
111 Fuselage bottom longeron
112 Wing root trailing-edge fillet
113 Radio and electrical system ground socket
114 Trailing-edge flap shroud ribs
115 Rear wing spar
116 Radiator shutter jack
117 Aileron cable runs
118 Gun heater air duct
119 Flap hydraulic jack
120 Flap synchronising jack
121 Port split trailing-edge flap
122 Aileron control bellcrank
123 Aileron hinge control rod
124 Port aileron construction
125 Wing tip construction
126 Port navigation light
127 Wing lattice rib construction
128 Front spar
129 Browning 0·303-in (7,7-mm) machine guns

130 Ammunition boxes (350 rounds per gun)
131 Machine gun muzzle blast tubes
132 Machine gun ports (patched)
133 Leading-edge nose ribs
134 Ammunition box armour protection
135 Cannon ammunition box (120 rounds)
136 Port 20-mm Hispano cannon
137 Ammunition feed drum
138 Cannon wing fairing
139 Cannon barrel
140 "C"-wing outboard cannon muzzle fairing (blanked-off)
141 Recoil spring
142 Inboard leading-edge lattice ribs

Supermarine Spitfire

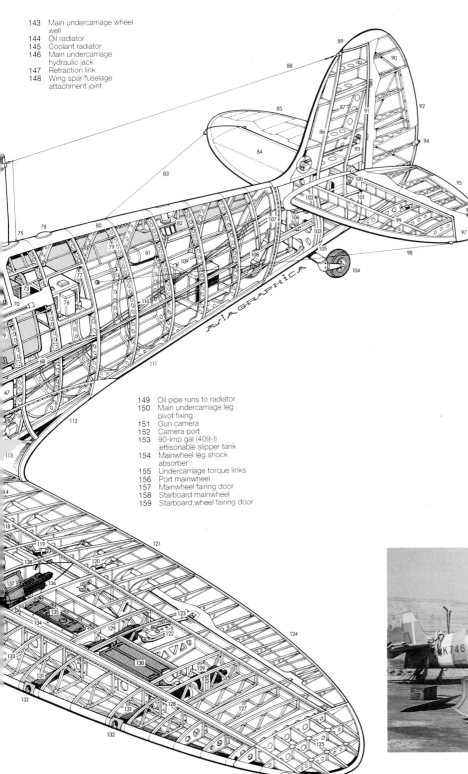

143 Main undercarriage wheel well
144 Oil radiator
145 Coolant radiator
146 Main undercarriage hydraulic jack
147 Retraction link
148 Wing spar/fuselage attachment joint

149 Oil pipe runs to radiator
150 Main undercarriage leg pivot fixing
151 Gun camera
152 Camera port
153 90-Imp gal (409-l) jettisonable slipper tank
154 Mainwheel leg shock absorber
155 Undercarriage torque links
156 Port mainwheel
157 Mainwheel fairing door
158 Starboard mainwheel
159 Starboard wheel fairing door

The event that was to overtake the development of the MkVIII was the emergence late in 1941 of the German Focke-Wulf FW 190. This new radial-engined fighter outclassed the Spitfire V by a wide margin. Trials between a captured FW 190A-3 and a Spitfire VB showed that the German fighter was at least 20mph (32km/hr) faster at all altitudes; it had better rates of climb and acceleration; it could dive faster initially; and, except in radius of turn, it was far more manoeuvrable. The Spitfire V took a heavy beating, and an urgent solution was needed. The MkVIII had been ordered in quantity, but it would not be available quickly enough. The answer was to fit the Merlin 60 series engine into a MkVC airframe. This became the Spitfire IX: the second most widely used variant, total production of which reached 5,609 aircraft of all subtypes. Produced in LF. (the most numerous), F. and HF. subtypes, the MkIX had a performance very close to that of the FW 190A-3: slightly worse in transient performance but better in the turn. The only difference between subtypes was the Merlin fitted; there were no external differences. From the air, the MkIX was

Below: Making the most of the time between sorties, engineers work on problems with the Rolls-Royce Merlin 61 engine in this Spitfire IX.

Developing the Breed

Left: Manufacture of the Spitfire was centred upon the Castle Bromwich Aircraft Factory (CBAF), as these factory-fresh MkIXs testify.

indistinguishable from the MkVC, and the German fighter pilots could not tell just what they were up against until combat was actually under way.

The Spitfire IX was still widely used at the end of the war, many examples being fitted with the E-wing. This carried a single .50 machine-gun in place of the two .303s. The 20mm cannon was retained. With the advent of the Griffon-engined Spitfire, the MkIX was largely devoted to low-level attack missions; a role for which its wings were frequently clipped. In later production aircraft, the large rudder became standard, and a 72 Imp gal (327.3 litre) fuel tank was installed in the rear fuselage of some examples. It is generally accepted that the Spitfire VIIIs and IXs were the last of the "ladies"; the next generation were not so nicely behaved, as ever-increasing power and weight took their toll of the Spitfire's previously docile handling qualities.

The next Spitfire in the numerical sequence was the PR.X. A total of 16 aircraft were converted from HF.VII airframes, which resulted in delivery being delayed until April 1944 due to the

SPECIFICATION

Spitfire F.IXC

Dimensions
Length: early examples 31ft 0½in (9.47m); late examples 31ft 4½in (9.57m)
Height: 12ft 7in (3.86m)
Wing span: 36ft 10in (11.23m)
Gross wing area: 242sq ft (22.44m^2)

Weights
Empty: 5,610lb (2,547kg)
Normal take-off weight: 7,500lb (3,405kg)
Overload weight: 9,500lb (4,313kg)

Power
1 × Rolls-Royce Merlin 61/63/63A liquid-cooled 12-cylinder Vee piston engine rated at 1,565, 1,650 and 1,650bhp respectively
Internal fuel: 85 Imp gal (386 litres)

External fuel: Provision made for carriage of drop tanks ranging from 30 to 170 Imp gal (136 to 773 litres)

Performance
Maximum speed: 408mph (656km/h) at 25,000ft (7,625m)
Cruising speed: 324mph (521km/h) at 20,000ft (6,100m)
Stalling speed (normal loaded weight): 86mph (138km/h) with flaps and undercarriage raised; 76mph (122km/h) with flaps and undercarriage lowered
Maximum rate of climb: 4,100ft/min (1,251m/min)
Service ceiling: 43,000ft (13,115m)
Typical mission range: 434 miles (698km)

Above: Several Spitfires were used to test the validity of a floatplane fighter, including this converted LF.IXB which first flew in 1944.

Above: A Spitfire IXB as operated by No.340 Sqn, Free French Air Force, during 1944–45. Early-production

MkIXs, such as this aircraft, had a rounded fin tip, whereas later examples had a more pointed unit.

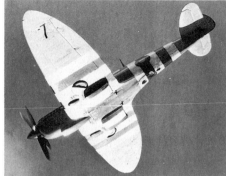

Above: Clearly evident in this view of a Spitfire PR.XI is the deeper engine cowling, which housed a larger oil tank, and the two under-fuselage apertures identifying the location of the vertical cameras.

Above: Combining an HF.VII airframe with wings from the PR.XI resulted in the PR.X for reconnaissance

work. This distinctively painted example served with Nos.541 and 542 Sqns, RAF, late in the war.

unavailability of suitable airframes. Powered by the high-altitude rated Merlin 64, the PR.X featured the wings of the earlier PR.XI, and a larger oil tank which deepened the underside of the nose

cowling. No armament was carried, and some of the armour protection was removed. The PR.X was not a great success, and was withdrawn from front-line service in September 1945.

Confusingly, the original MkIV, later redesignated the MkXX, became the prototype MkXII: the first of the Griffon-engined production Spitfires. Yet another interim type, the MkXII was intended to counter high-speed, hit-and-run raids at low-level by German fighters. Production totalled just 100. The Griffon rotated the opposite way to the Merlin, producing a strong swing to the right on take-off, a feature that was not helped by the asymmetric radiator, located beneath the star-

Above: The single MkVIII Trainer was followed by the conversion of 20 MkIX airframes as two-seat trainers known as T.IXs.

PR DERIVATIVE

The PR.XI was chronologically well ahead of the PR.X, being derived from the MkIX, and 471 were built. Powered by a Merlin 70, it could climb to 44,000ft (13,420m) and attain a speed of 422mph (679km/hr). The only MkIX derivative to have a retractable tailwheel, the PR.XI had the broad chord rudder; an enlarged oil tank like all PR variants; and the same leading-edge fuel tanks in the wings pioneered by the PR.IV, bringing the total fuel capacity up to 228 Imp gals (1,036 litres). Deliveries commenced in late 1942, early aircraft being powered by the Merlin 60 series engine.

Above: Under the watchful eye of the pilot, one of the two F.52 vertical cameras is loaded into the fuselage via the rear fuselage access panel.

Developing the Breed

board wing. Entering service in June 1943, the clipped-wing Spitfire XII proved generally superior to the contemporary models of the FW 190A at low level. Engines for this variant were the Griffon III and IV, and about half the number built had a retractable tailwheel, while almost all examples had the pointed fin and rudder.

LOW-LEVEL RECCE

The next Spitfire in the production sequence was the PR.XIII. This was a departure from previous reconnaissance machines; whereas all previous PR Spitfires had been intended to snoop unarmed at high altitude, the PR.XIII was intended to operate at low level in the tactical reconnaissance role. Due to the higher risk of interception, the A-wing was fitted, with two machine-guns per wing. Two vertical and one oblique cameras were carried. A total of 25 PR.XIIIs were acquired, converted mainly from MkV airframes and powered by the Merlin 32. The survivors were withdrawn as obsolete early in 1945.

The most potent member of the family to be used during the Second World War was the Spitfire XIV, which was based on

Below: This view of a Spitfire XIV shows the five-bladed propeller, as well as the large and symmetrical underwing radiators necessary due to the use of an intercooler.

Above: The distinctive lines of the engine cowling identify this as a Griffon-powered Spitfire, more specifically a Spitfire XII – the first model to feature the Griffon in preference to the Merlin.

Above: Also powered by the Griffon engine, this Spitfire FR.XIV sports a distinctive teardrop canopy and a cut-down rear fuselage. Following service with the RAF, this example was supplied to India.

the MkVIII airframe strengthened to take the Griffon 65, rated at 2,035hp. Like the Merlin, the Griffon had been fitted with a two-stage supercharger, and a five-bladed propeller was used to convert the power of this engine into thrust. The fin area was increased and an enlarged pointed rudder fitted to improve what would otherwise have been marginal directional stability, and the overall fuselage length increased. Fuel capacity was 115 Imp gals (522.7 litres). Maximum speed rose to 439mph (706km/hr), rate of climb to 4,700ft/min (1,433.5m/min), and service ceiling to 43,000ft (13,115m). Takeoff weight had risen to 8,750lb (3,972.5kg), and the flight controls were correspondingly heavy by comparison with earlier Spitfires. On the other hand, the MkXIV looked far tougher and more workmanlike when it entered service in October 1944. Surprisingly, it was more manoeuvrable than the much lighter MkVIII at all altitudes, mainly due to the ability of the Griffon to haul it around corners at high angles of attack, even though below 20,000ft (6,100m) maximum speeds were much the same. If it had a fault, it was that its terminal velocity was limited to 470mph (756km/hr). This was due to control problems caused by "aileron float", and was never entirely cured, despite numerous attempts. Early models mounted the C-wing, but the

majority carried the E-wing with two .50 machine-guns replacing the four .303 Brownings. Later production models sported a cut-down rear fuselage and a bubble canopy. A further model carried a fuselage camera in the tactical reconnaissance role; this was the FR.XIVE, which had clipped wing tips. This was also the first Spitfire variant to carry the gyro gunsight.

There was no Spitfire XV or XVII, these designations being applied to Seafires, of which more later. The next in numerical order was the Spitfire XVI. This was for all practical purposes a MkIX powered by a Packard-built Merlin 266. As this was not interchangeable with the Rolls-Royce article, a new mark number was issued to avoid confusion. In all, 1,054 F.XVIs and LF.XVIs were built, the latter sporting the clipped E-wing. From early 1945, they were produced with a bubble canopy and the taller pointed rudder. Entering service fairly late in the war, most were to be used in the ground-attack role.

POST-WAR MODELS

The Spitfire XVIII, which was an upgraded MkXIV, was destined to become the final development of the original airframe. Just too late for the war, 100 were built in the F(fighter) and 200 in the FR (fighter-reconnaissance) configurations, the latter with three vertical cameras. Additional fuel tanks were installed in the wings and rear fuselage, increasing total capacity to 175.5 Imp gal (798 litres) in the F.XVIII to give longer range. The FR.XVIII carried rather less fuel, due to the cameras occupying tankage space. The cut-down rear fuselage and bubble canopy were standard on this variant, as was the E-wing. Once again, the fuselage and main landing gear had to be strengthened to cope with the extra weight, the maximum overload rising to no less than 11,000lb (4,994kg).

The PR.XIX was the last unarmed reconnaissance Spitfire variant, and 225

were built. The first 21 aircraft were unpressurized and powered by the Griffon 65, whereas the remainder were pressurized and powered by the Griffon 66, the wings on the latter having extra fuel tanks which increased total capacity to 172 Imp gals (782 litres). Otherwise, it was based on the MkXIV. Entering service just after the war's end, this model made its last operational flight in Malaya on 1 April 1954.

The first major redesign of the basic Spitfire airframe had been the MkIII, and this was continued with the MkVIII. Next came the Mk21. Lateral control problems with the MkXIV had made it clear that a new wing was needed if worthwhile advances were to be made. Greater stiffness was required, and larger ailerons were fitted to improve the aircraft's rate of roll. These were about 8in (20cm) longer than the originals, and this made it necessary to straighten the trailing-edge near

the wing tip, with the result that the span increased by one inch and the area by two square feet $(0.19m^2)$. The wing planform was still a flattened ellipse, but with squarer tips. Small extra fuel tanks were built into the wings, which carried two 20mm Hispano each side as standard. Ground handling, always a problem in the Spitfire, was improved by spacing the main landing gear legs a few inches farther apart, and these were lengthened to give clearance for a larger-diameter propeller. Power was provided by the same Griffon 61 as used by the MkXIV, but the big propeller gave the Mk21 a speed advantage over the MkXIV at all altitudes. The weight of armour increased to 190lb (86kg), and normal take-off weight to 9,124lb (4,142kg). The fuselage was strengthened to cope accordingly, mainly by means of four stainless steel longerons, and the empennage was also redesigned. With all these changes, the

Above: With the exception of its Packard-built Merlin 266 engine, the Spitfire XVI was essentially a MkIX. Over 1,000 were to be built, including this No.74 Sqn, RAF, LF.XVIC, complete with bombs.

Above: Too late to be "blooded" in the Second World War, the MkXVIII featured additional fuel tanks in the wings and fuselage. The tell-tale camera port behind the cockpit identifies this as an FR.XVIII.

Developing the Breed

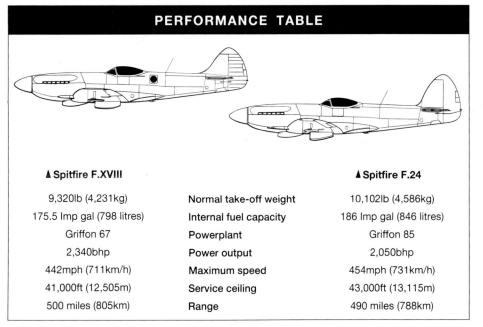
Spitfire 21 was virtually a new aeroplane, and many modifications had to be made before it was accepted for service in March 1945. A total of 122 Mk21s were built, some of the later aircraft sporting the Griffon 85 with six-blade contra-rotating propellers.

Almost in parallel with the Spitfire 21 was the Mk22, which was to become the mainstay of the Royal Auxiliary Air Force's (RAuxAF) squadrons from 1946 until 1952. The main differences between these models were that the latter had a cut-down rear fuselage and bubble canopy as standard, and a new empennage which had been developed for the Supermarine Spiteful, which gave an increase in both horizontal and vertical tail surfaces of more than one quarter. Late-production Mk22s were powered by the Griffon 85 with a contra-rotating propeller. Altogether, 278 Mk22s were built.

As early as 1942, it had become obvious that the Spitfire suffered from excessive drag rise at high speeds, and that much of this arose from the wing camber. A new high-speed section was developed and fitted to the prototype Mk21 to become the

Mk23. This variant, known also as the Super Spitfire, or the Valiant, featured an enlarged fin, with the leading-edge raked sharply forward. But by this time, the prototype Spiteful with a laminar-flow wing had already flown, rendering the Mk23 operationally obsolescent.

FINAL CHAPTER

The final Spitfire variant was the Mk24, of which only 54 were delivered. Almost identical to the Mk22, it featured only minor changes, such as short-barrelled 20mm Hispano MkV cannon, and had the Spiteful-type tail assembly as standard. The ultimate Spitfire, it could hit 454mph (730km/hr), had a service ceiling of 43,000ft (13,115m) and a maximum rate of climb of 4,900ft/min (1,494.5m/min), and on test was dived at 525mph (844.7km/hr) with no problems. Compared with the Spitfire I, the empty weight had risen by 70 per cent to 7,351lb (3,337kg), take-off weight by 63 per cent to 10,102lb (4,586kg), and maximum overload to a massive 12,150lb (5,516kg). Internal fuel capacity had risen by a

massive 119 per cent to 186 Imp gals (845.5 litres), and the power had also more than doubled. The Spitfire 24 was 25 per cent faster, could fly 34 per cent higher and climbed nearly twice as fast. But by the time that this was achieved, the jet fighter had rendered such achievements all but obsolete.

The sorry performance of carrierborne fighters in the early years of the war made it almost inevitable that the Spitfire would be pressed into service, although its endurance was really too limited for effective naval operations, and its closely-spaced main landing gear not really suitable for carrier landings. In its navalized form, the Spitfire was known, very appropriately, as the Seafire.

The first Seafire was the MkIB, a converted Spitfire MkVB fitted with a tailhook for arrested landings, points for slinging, and instruments calibrated in knots. A total of 166 were delivered, commencing in June 1942. Then came the Seafire IIC, followed by the clipped-wing L.IIC for low-altitude work, this last mounting the Merlin 32 with a four-bladed propeller. All later Seafire IIs were fitted with spools for catapult-launching, and could be adapted for rocket-assisted take-off (RATO). A total of 400 Seafire IICs were built, the final variant being a fighter-reconnaissance aircraft equipped with one vertical and one oblique camera.

The first Seafires all had fixed wings, which made it impossible for them to use the lifts on the Royal Navy (RN) carriers then in service. The obvious next step was to produce a folding-wing aircraft which could be stored below deck. The result was the Seafire III, in which the wings folded upwards outside the wheel wells; the tips then folded downwards to reduce the headroom required. Folding had to be done manually, and this took five men. Power was provided by the Merlin 55 in the standard fighter version, and the Merlin 55M in the LF.III, which was the most numerous variant of the 1,200 built. Some early-production aircraft had the bulky Vokes tropical filter. Performance

Above: Virtually identical to the Spitfire 21, the Mk22, of which 278 were built, was to serve primarily with units of the Royal Auxiliary Air Force (RAuxAF). A No.603 Sqn aircraft is illustrated here.

Like the Spitfire, later-production Seafires had the Spiteful-type tail. Total builds were 50 Mk45s and 24 Mk46s, but neither model entered front-line service.

The final Seafire variant was the Mk47, which was the fully-navalized version of the Spitfire 24, with wings that folded at a single point outboard of the wheel wells. The Griffon 85, with a six-bladed contra-rotating prop, powered all Mk47s, and all had the Spiteful-type empennage. Externally, it was very similar to the Seafire 46, but could be distinguished by the intake lip just below the spinner, and the short-barrelled 20mm cannons. Most examples of this model were configured with cameras as FR.47s. Only 90 were built, the last being delivered in 1949.

While the Seafire was a formidable opponent in air combat, it was never really suited to carrierborne operations. The lady was too genteel for the nasty, rough sailors, and accidents accounted for far more casualties than enemy action. The view over the nose was totally inadequate for safe carrier landings, and endurance was always too short for effective fleet operations, in which extended combat air patrols and long-range escort are mandatory, as are far greater safety margins than are customary in land-based operations.

Above: A mere 54 examples of what was destined to become the final variant of the Spitfire family, the Mk24, were built for post-war use. Note the rocket projectiles on the underwing racks of this machine.

was much improved over the MkII, and the Seafire III, including a fighter-reconnaissance version, was still in front-line service at the end of the war.

The Seafire XV entered service just too late to see action in the Pacific. Powered by the Griffon MkVI, rated at 1,750hp, the MkXV had much in common with the Spitfire XIV, including the broad-chord fin and pointed rudder. A total of 384 Seafire XVs were built.

NAVAL DEVELOPMENT

The Seafire XVII was an updated MkXV, and featured a cut-down fuselage and bubble canopy. It was to be built in two versions, fighter and fighter-reconnaissance, and had considerable structural strengthening, notably to the main wing spar and chassis. The stroke of the oleo legs had been increased, which reduced the bounce problems in an arrested landing,

and it carried more fuel than the MkXV. It had a short operational life, however, serving with front-line squadrons for less than two years.

The Seafire 45 was a semi-navalized version of the Spitfire 21, with sting hook and a tailwheel guard to protect it against the arrester wires. Its wings were fixed, but the lifts on fleet carriers were rather larger than they had been. The Seafire 45 was powered by the Griffon 61 with a five-bladed propeller, or the Griffon 85 with a contra-rotating propeller. Standard armament was four 20mm cannon. The Seafire 46 was similarly based on the Spitfire 22, with cut-down fuselage and bubble canopy, and with the same engines and modifications as the Mk45.

Right: Storage space aboard aircraft carriers is always at a premium, so a wing-folding mechanism for the Seafire was all but mandatory.

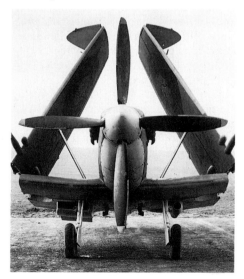

A FIGHTER is essentially a flying gun platform, and it is designed for just one purpose – to bring guns to bear on an enemy as expeditiously as possible. During the First World War, and for many years after, the universal fighter weapon was the rifle-calibre machine-gun. At first just one gun was carried, then two; by the early-1930s, engine power had increased to the point where four guns could be carried with only a marginal loss of performance. It was possible for even larger-calibre guns to be carried, which provided greatly increased single-strike hitting power, but the penalties were severe. Gun for gun, they were much heavier and more difficult to accommodate within the constraints of the contemporary fighter designs, both of which penalized the fighter's performance. They were sensitive to vibration unless rigidly mounted on the heavy structure close to the engine, and local strengthening might be needed to absorb the recoil. The larger the calibre, the slower the rate of fire, thus the hit potential would be less; and less ammunition could be carried, which shortened firing time and reduced combat persistence. Given all of these factors, plus plenty of suitable ammunition already in stock, it is little wonder that the .303in calibre machine-gun was selected to arm the Spitfire.

At first the specification to which the Spitfire was a response called for the fitment of four machine-guns. This figure was later increased to six, then finally eight. How this came about is a long story. Back in 1933, Squadron Leader (later Sir) Ralph Sorley took charge of the Operational Requirements section at the Air Ministry. Previously a pilot, he had spent a great deal of time in the slow biplanes of the day, shooting at, and mostly missing, aerial targets. His assessment was that the average squadron pilot was unable to

hold the gunsight on the target for more than two seconds. With the speeds of both bombers and fighters increasing rapidly, the time available for an average burst of fire might become even shorter. Greater firepower was obviously needed.

During 1934, the Air Ministry evaluated many different types of aircraft guns, finally choosing the American 0.30in

Above: With its impressive firepower and excellent rate of turn, finding a Spitfire on his tail, lining up for an attack, was something every Luftwaffe fighter pilot dreaded.

calibre Colt machine-gun as its standard weapon. It was to be produced under licence by the Birmingham Small Arms

Supermarine Spitfire

Whereas the thick-winged Hurricane had its guns closely grouped in banks of four, the guns on the Spitfire were widely spaced, due to the need for the ammunition boxes to be accommodated alongside them. The theoretical effective range of the Browning .303 was 3,000ft (914m), but the limiting factor was the marksmanship of the pilot. At first the guns were harmonized to give even coverage over a large area of sky at a distance of 1,350ft (411.7m), on the assumption that some hits would be scored on a target within the square. This penalized those few pilots who could actually shoot straight, and combat experience soon led to all guns being harmonized on a point some 900ft (274.5m) ahead. Some of the more expert marksmen preferred point-harmonization of the guns at a range of 450ft (137m).

The types of .303 ammunition generally used were ball, armour-piercing (AP), incendiary and tracer. Normally, two guns were loaded with AP, two with incendiary and four with ball, although

Above: The MkVB replaced the MkVA in production, bringing an increase in firepower courtesy of a mix of .303in machine-guns and 20mm cannon, as illustrated by this aircraft serving with the RAF.

Above: Built at Castle Bromwich, this Spitfire F.VB served with RAF and RAAF squadrons, before being issued to the USAAF's 67th Reconnaissance Group. Note how the 20mm cannon protrudes well forward of the wing.

Below: A recently-completed Spitfire IIA in the markings of No.66 Sqn, RAF, with the original armament configuration of four .303in machine guns per wing.

factory, and be known as the Browning .303. It was a fairly light and compact weapon with a rate of fire of approximately 1,150 rounds per minute, and a muzzle velocity of 2,400ft/sec (732m/sec), both of which were far better than the Vickers gun that it succeeded. Working with ballistics expert F.W. Hill, Sorley calculated that roughly 300 bullets would need to be fired in order to achieve sufficient hits to destroy a bomber. To do this in the space of two seconds would require eight Brownings. These were to be mounted in the wings of the new monoplane fighters, firing outside the propeller disc. A more central location would have been preferable from an aiming point of view, but then synchronization gears would have been needed to avoid damage to the propeller blades. This would have involved more weight, greater complexity and yet another subsystem to take up valuable engine power, as well as a reduction in the rate of fire. A belt of 300 rounds

was provided for each gun, giving just under 16 seconds of firing time, or the equivalent of eight two-second bursts. This was later increased to 350 rounds of ammunition per gun.

Firepower

Above: Accurate gun harmonization and alignment is crucial for any fighter. Here work is carried out on a USAAF Spitfire VB. Note the target board in the background.

there were many exceptions. Four tracer bullets were included in the final 25 rounds of each belt of ball ammunition to warn the pilot that he was nearing the end of the belt. Widely used was De Wilde AP incendiary ammunition, which gave a flash on hitting the target, thus confirming that the pilot's aim was accurate. This was normally included at one in every five rounds, but a few pilots had their guns loaded with one round of De Wilde to one round of ball. This was a dirty loading, however, and quickly led to the fouling of the gun barrels.

LINE OF FIRE

Aiming was done with the GM 2 reflector gunsight, in which a circle of light with a central dot (a combination known as the graticule) was projected onto a screen in front of the pilot. Running horizontally across the circle was a broken line, the break in the middle of which could be adjusted in the air to suit the wingspans of various adversary aircraft. This told the pilot when he was in firing range. Focussed at infinity, it was easy for the pilot to see the sight while watching his opponent

at the same time. This distance between the dot and the ring represented a 50mph (80km/hr) crossing speed as an aid to deflection shooting. The gunsight's luminosity could be adjusted to suit the prevailing light conditions, and it offered an added advantage in that, unless the pilot's head was in the right position, he was unable to see the graticule.

Even before the start of the Second World War greater hitting power was being sought. The weapon selected was the 20mm Hispano Suiza cannon, which displaced the Spitfire's two innermost

Below: With the wing access panel removed, RAF groundcrew prepare to install an ammunition drum for one of the aircraft's 20mm Hispano-Suiza cannon.

Brownings. The Hispano was a very powerful weapon, spitting out shells at a muzzle velocity of 2,820ft/sec (860m/sec), at the rate of 700 per minute. These figures bettered those of all wartime German 20mm cannon designs.

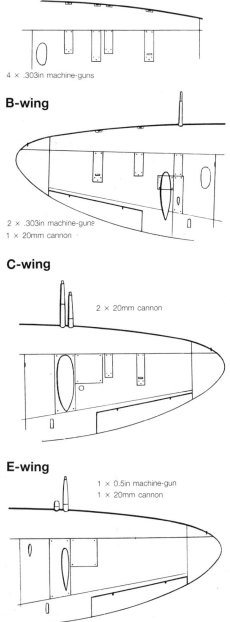

A-wing
4 × .303in machine-guns

B-wing
2 × .303in machine-guns
1 × 20mm cannon

C-wing
2 × 20mm cannon

E-wing
1 × 0.5in machine-gun
1 × 20mm cannon

Early Spitfire cannon were supplied by a drum magazine holding 60 rounds, giving just over five seconds of firing time. This was later increased to 11 seconds when a belt feed of 120 rounds became available. From 1942, many Spitfires were produced with four cannon, although two of these were often removed as the hitting power of a pair was found to be adequate for most purposes. Ball, AP and high-explosive (HE) incendiary shells were used in conjunction with the Hispano cannon. Of these, both ball and AP were found to be most effective against aircraft, as on impact they penetrated deep, the energy of the shell being released as red heat, igniting any inflammable material(s) it came into contact with.

Whereas the firing button for the Spitfire's machine-gun armament had been a circular button on the pilot's control column, the mixed armament configuration needed a double-square firing button. Central pressure fired all the

Below: A significant improvement in target tracking was offered by the adoption of a gyroscopic gunsight.

Above: A Spitfire XIV operated by No.610 Sqn, RAF, one of 11 units tasked with patrolling England's south coast and the English Channel to intercept incoming German V1 flying bombs during 1944–45.

Above: The Spitfire 21 could pack quite a punch, thanks to its tally of four 20mm cannon. The ammunition for each cannon was fed through in belts, these having replaced earlier smaller-capacity drums.

guns: top pressure for machine-guns only, bottom pressure for cannon only.

EXTRA PUNCH

The final type of gun carried by the Spitfire was the Colt-Browning .50 calibre heavy machine-gun, which was introduced in conjunction with the E-type wing. Rate of fire was 850 rounds per minute, and muzzle velocity 2,790ft/sec (851m/sec). The projectile was almost exactly four times heavier than that of the .303, and had exceptional ballistic qualities. Fitted to the E-wing, the new gun replaced the two inner Browning .303s, with the Hispano 20mm cannon being carried outside them. A belt of 250 rounds per gun was carried, giving almost 18 seconds of firing time. The .50 was effective over much longer ranges than either of the other gun types and had a rather greater weight of fire than two .303s, but was still limited by the ability of the pilot to aim straight. Throughout the entire war, neither the Germans nor the Japanese armoured their aircraft to withstand hits from the .50 machine-gun.

The average squadron pilot could hit a non-evading target quite consistently from within an angle not exceeding 15deg of the tail, but manoeuvring targets were quite a different matter. This state of affairs was improved from late-1943, when the gyroscopic gunsight entered service. The display on the reflector glass showed a ring of six diamonds, the width of which was adjustable to suit the wingspan of an opponent, along with a central pipper. As the pilot tracked the target, the mechanism would cause the display to move about to give the deflection shooting angle required. This effectively doubled the marksmanship of the average pilot, although the real marksmen who had already mastered the art of deflection shooting on the old fixed graticule sight gained little benefit from it.

THE Spitfire was designed as a quick-reaction, agile, short-range interceptor for the air defence of the British Isles; and this is how it was used during the first years of the Second World War. Its combat debut came on 16 October 1939, when nine Luftwaffe Junkers Ju 88 bombers attacked British warships in the Firth of Forth, Scotland. Spitfires from Nos. 602 and 603 Squadrons intercepted, shooting down two Ju 88s and damaging a third, for no loss. It was an encouraging start to the Spitfire's career.

The first clashes between the Spitfire and its German counterpart, the Messerschmitt Bf 109E, came over Dunkirk, France, on 23 May 1940. Later that same day, an epic low-level fight took place between two Spitfires of No.54 Squadron

Below: Though the Spitfire did not have it all its own way when it came to taking on Luftwaffe fighters, this photograph is believed to be a fake produced by Germany for propaganda.

Above: A gaggle of No.65 Squadron, RAF, Spitfire Is photographed over the English countryside in mid-1939, shortly before the outbreak of the Second World War.

and a dozen Bf 109Es. Three German fighters were shot down, for one Spitfire damaged; an engagement that convinced the British that the Spitfire was superior to the Bf 109 in nearly every department. This was not quite true; at altitudes above 20,000ft (6,100m) the performance of the German fighter was in some respects the better of the two. Also, both of the Spitfires involved were fitted with the Rotol constant-speed propeller, which gave them a better rate of climb than the two-speed propeller fitted to the majority of early-production Spitfires.

For nearly two weeks, British fighters flew continuous patrols to cover the evacuation from Dunkirk, often penetrating inland to intercept the German bombers before they could reach their targets. Far from their bases, the time the British squadrons could spend in enemy territory was limited, and they were often outnumbered. In the ferocious fighting that took place, the Luftwaffe pilots quickly learned to respect the Spitfire.

THE FEW

Dunkirk was followed by the Battle of Britain, and it was in this campaign that the Spitfire earned its immortal fame. Day after day, the defending fighters faced massive waves of German bombers heavily escorted by fighters, interspersed with large-scale fighter sweeps and the occasional sneak raid at low-level. As it was virtually impossible to deflect a major raid from its target, the RAF's aims were fourfold. Firstly, to reduce the effects of the Luftwaffe raids by disrupting the bomber formations. Secondly, to inflict a high level of attrition on the attackers. Thirdly, to reduce the morale of the Luftwaffe by mounting a consistently determined defence. Fourthly, to remain in being as an effective fighting force In all these they succeeded. There was also a fifth factor which is all too rarely given sufficient recognition. Efficient warfare depends largely on good intelligence,

Above: The Dornier Do 17 may have been faster than previous biplane bombers, but it was still vulnerable to the attentions of the Spitfire.

which relies to a great extent on reconnaissance. On every morning of the Battle, Luftwaffe reconnaissance aircraft crossed the British coast, and on every occasion the British fighters harassed them, shot them down, and finally drove them to seek safety at altitudes where the definition of their cameras was inadequate for the task. The fast-climbing, high-flying Spitfire interceptors fulfilled this function admirably.

Mere statistics cannot account for the reputation gained by the Spitfire during the Battle of Britain. No less than 19 of the single-engined, single-seat fighter squadrons deployed in the Battle were equipped with Spitfires: some 38 per cent of the total. Spitfires flew roughly two-fifths of all sorties, and shot down German aircraft in much the same proportion.

Below: As the Battle of Britain raged on through the summer months of 1940, Spitfire-equipped units played a decisive role in defending mainland Britain. One such unit was No.610 Sqn, based Biggin Hill.

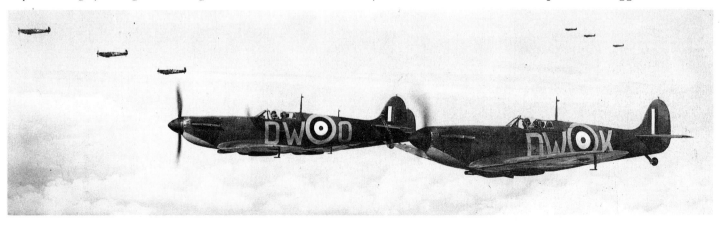

The Missions

DEPLOYMENT

**RAF Fighter Command Spitfire Squadrons
August 1940**

Sqn	Base
19	Fowlmere
41	Catterick
54	Hornchurch
64	Kenley
65	Hornchurch
66	Coltishall
72	Acklington
74	Hornchurch
92	Pembrey
152	Warmwell
222	Kirton
234	St. Eval
266	Eastchurch
602	Drem
603	Montrose/Dyce
609	Middle Wallop
610	Biggin Hill
611	Digby
616	Leconfield

Below: As the Battle of Britain wore on, Luftwaffe losses mounted as RAF Fighter Command began to turn the tide. Here, Canadian and French Spitfire pilots chalk up the 1,000th "kill" in the Biggin Hill sector.

At the height of the Battle, during August and September 1940, Spitfire combat losses accounted for 36 per cent of the total; while of those fighters damaged too badly to be repaired at base, Spitfires accounted for nearly half: a higher proportion than should have been expected. So in bare figures, the combat record of the Spitfire was not significantly better than that of the Hurricane. How then did it gain such a formidable reputation?

The answer lies in the way in which the Battle of Britain was fought. Before the RAF fighter squadrons were scrambled, their ground controllers had to be certain that the incoming raid was not a feint, or a fighter sweep, designed to put the defenders at a disadvantage. Consequently, they were often sent off late, with insufficient time to gain an altitude advantage. Furthermore, their main objective was to shoot down bombers, and attempts to do this almost invariably made them vulnerable to the German escort fighters. Under these circumstances one would expect little difference in the combat results between the Spitfire and the Hurricane, one being just as vulnerable as the other to return fire from German bombers, or a Bf 109 swooping onto its tail. But there

Above: The chances of a Luftwaffe Heinkel He 111 bomber managing to get on a Spitfire's tail must have been few and far between, but this propaganda shot shows just that.

was yet another factor involved. Where possible, the superior Spitfire was directed to engage the German escort fighters, thus leaving the way clear for the Hurricane-equipped squadrons to get at the bombers. This the Spitfire squadrons did, usually at a distinct tactical disadvantage. Bearing in mind this tremendous handicap, the achievements of the Spitfire during the Battle of Britain were remarkable.

A WINNING EDGE

In combat, the Spitfire's greatest advantages over the Bf 109 were its faster roll rate and its ability to turn more tightly. These capabilities allowed it to evade an attack and get out of the line of fire quickly. They also enabled the Spitfire to turn in behind an enemy aircraft and stay in a firing position during hard manoeuvres. In theory, this greater manoeuvrability allowed the Spitfire to outfight the Bf 109E in one-on-one combat. Alas, warfare is not so straightforward, and staying after one opponent for too long leaves the attacker vulnerable. However, it was still enough of an advantage to worry the German fighter leaders badly. Some indication of the problem is given in a letter home written by a young German fighter

Supermarine Spitfire

Above: The Royal Observer Corps presented a pair of Spitfire IIAs to the RAF during 1940, this being the first of the two. It was flown by No.41 Sqn, RAF, until late-1940, but was lost in action in 1941.

Above: The Spitfire was to be used extensively in support of the Allied campaigns in Southern Europe and North Africa. This MkVB served with the South African Air Force (SAAF) in Italy during 1943.

pilot: "Often the Spitfires give beautiful displays of aerobatics. Recently, I had to watch in admiration as one of them played a game with thirty Messerschmitts, without itself ever getting into danger . . ." Werner Moelders and Adolf Galland, two of the Luftwaffe's great fighter aces, met early in the Battle to discuss how best to counter the British fighter. They decided that the only effective way in which they could offset the superior manoeuvrability of the Spitfire was to adopt dive-and-zoom tactics, never turning with it for long enough to lose the advantages conferred by superior tactical position, numbers and a better rate of climb. Taking these factors into consideration, it seems reasonable to assume that the Spitfires had the harder part of the Battle, and that without them the Hurricanes would have suffered even more heavily than they did.

Such was the impression that the Spitfire made, that the Luftwaffe suffered from "Spitfire snobbery", their pilots being reluctant to admit to having been given a hard time by Hurricanes, and even more reluctant to admit being shot down by one! Six of the top-scoring British squadrons in the Battle flew Spitfires, as did more than half of the 27 pilots who scored ten or more victories.

The Spitfire was evaluated as a night fighter during the summer of 1940, but to no avail. A few lucky "kills" were scored, but it was not really a suitable platform for the task. Baffles were fitted between the exhausts and the pilot's line of sight in an attempt to minimize the blinding effect of the exhaust flames, but with no electronic detection aids, the programme was doomed to failure.

The year 1941 saw Spitfires taking the fight to the enemy; "leaning forward into France", as Sholto Douglas, the new Commander-in-Chief of RAF Fighter Command, put it. The cannon-armed Spitfire V entered service, and this proved to be an excellent match for the new Bf 109F. In an operation known as a "Circus", half a dozen RAF bombers would be despatched to targets in northern France, escorted by up to 22 squadrons of Spitfires. The role of the bombers was primarily to act as "bait" to bring the defending Luftwaffe fighters into battle. These operations achieved little, although it must be said that the manoeuvrability of the Spitfire made it more effective in the close escort role than the Bf 109E had been the previous summer. When, in 1942,

Below: The Battle of Britain had been won, and Spitfires were soon to be operating from their British bases against targets in mainland Europe.

The Missions

Above: The arrival of the Focke-Wulf FW 190 was to dramatically improve the Luftwaffe's fighter force, and challenge the Spitfire's aerial supremacy over Europe.

the German Focke-Wulf FW 190 entered service in large numbers, the Spitfire V no longer reigned supreme, and losses began to mount. As related earlier, the Spitfire IX was rushed into service to redress the balance of air superiority. "Circus" operations were to account for the majority of Spitfire sorties over the next two years, its short combat range restricting it to relatively shallow penetrations over occupied territory, even when auxiliary underwing drop tanks were carried.

Second only to the Battle of Britain in the Spitfire story was the epic defence of Malta. The island was an "unsinkable aircraft carrier" placed astride the Axis lines of communication between Italy and North Africa, and as such, a great deal of effort was made by the Luftwaffe and the Italian Regia Aeronautica to neutralize it. Outnumbered, under constant air attack, short of spares, fuel and ammunition, the Malta-based Spitfires defended the island heroically against overwhelming odds, finally turning the tide in mid-1942. Casualties were high, and resupply was a constant problem. To solve this, Spitfires were flown to Malta off Royal Navy aircraft carriers by pilots who had rarely even seen a carrier before, over a distance of 660 miles (1,062km). To give them the

necessary endurance, they carried 90 Imp gal slipper tanks under their bellies, which did nothing to enhance their fighting qualities if they were engaged en route by Axis fighters operating from airfields in North Africa and the island of Pantellaria. Still later, Spitfires fitted with a 170 Imp gal (772.8 litre) slipper tank, a 30 Imp gal (136 litre) ferry tank in the rear fuselage and an extra oil tank, flew direct to Malta from Gibraltar, a distance of roughly 1,000 miles (1,609km).

FIGHTER-BOMBERS

It was also from Malta that the Spitfire first flew bombing missions. By mid-summer 1942, air superiority over the island had been gained, and fighter sweeps over Sicilian airfields were initiated. These were ignored by the German and Italian fighters, and improvised bomb racks were fitted to the Spitfires to provoke them into a reaction. A 250lb (113.5kg) bomb was carried under each wing, the pilot dropping them while in a steep dive, using the reflector gunsight to aim. Bomb-carrying Spitfires, known unofficially as "Spitbombers" or "Bombfires", were widely used in North Africa, Sicily, Italy and other theatres of operations. These were mainly the "clipped, clapped

Above: Nine fighter squadrons were assigned to the Northwest African Tactical Air Force during 1943, including the 308th Squadron, 31st Fighter Group, USAAF, equipped with Spitfire VCs.

Above: Nicknamed "Grey Nurse", this sharkmouthed MkVIII served with No.457 Sqn, RAAF, in the defence of Australia against the marauding Japanese fighters and bombers, including the Mitsubishi A6M Zero.

Supermarine Spitfire

Left: Royal Navy ratings and RAF ground crew work together to turn this Spitfire V around between missions in the defence of Malta. Note the profusion of fuel cans.

a few small-scale encounters in the first months of 1943, a large Japanese raid was intercepted over the Timor Sea. The Spitfire pilots got a nasty shock when they tried to out-turn the agile Zeros, and five Spitfires were lost for a score of five Zeros and a bomber. The Spitfire simply could not stay with a turning Zero at moderate-to-low speeds, and their pilots were forced to adopt dive-and-zoom tactics to counter future Japanese raids.

Spitfire VIIIs entered service late in 1943, and were used widely in Italy and the Balkans, as well as operating against Japanese forces in the Far East. They could outfight the German and Italian fighters, and enjoyed a considerable superiority of performance over the Japanese fighters of the period. They arrived in Burma early in 1944, shortly before the Kohima and Imphal battles began in March and April of that year. This was at a time when the Japanese

and cropped" Spitfire LF.VCs, which were also used for interdiction missions over Northern France from 1943. When a fighter escort was needed, it was often provided by Spitfire IXs.

Below: A highly versatile aircraft, the Spitfire could deliver a modest payload of bombs if necessary. Such aircraft were sometimes referred to as "Bombfires" or "Spitbombers" for very obvious reasons.

The nearest Japanese equivalent to the Spitfire was the Mitsubishi A6M Zero, which gained a fearsome reputation in the early years of the Second World War for its ability to turn on a yen. When the Japanese advance across the Pacific brought their bombers to within striking distance of the Australian mainland, a Wing of Spitfire VCs, consisting of No.54 Sqn, RAF, and Nos. 452 and 457 Sqns, Royal Australian Air Force (RAAF), were sent to Darwin to oppose them. After

Below: The pilot of this USAAF machine managed to open the side-hinged cockpit entry/exit door and escape after ditching while flying in support of Allied ground forces operating near Salerno, Italy.

The Missions

Above: Conditions in the Far East during the monsoon season were far from ideal, especially when it came to maintaining adequate runways!

fighter units in the region were wasting away, and little air opposition was encountered. Defensive patrolling, fighter sweeps, interdiction and close air support occupied most of the Spitfire's energies.

Meanwhile, back in Western Europe, 1943 had seen the service entry of the first Griffon-engined Spitfire: the optimized low-level F.XII fighter variant intended to counter tip-and-run raids on South Coast targets by the FW 190A. Issued only to Nos. 41 and 91 Sqns, the F.XII was also used for low-level, anti-shipping reconnaissance operations between The Hague, in the Netherlands, and Le Havre, in France, and air-sea rescue escort operations. The F.XII was followed into service in January 1944 by the superlative Spitfire XIV, which was to play such a decisive part in defeating the V 1 flying bombs, and later in gaining air superiority over the European continent. The Spitfire XIV was rather faster than the FW 190A at all operating heights, and had a better rate of sustained climb. Slightly better in the dive, it was greatly

superior in the turn. Only in its roll rate did the German fighter have the advantage. Against the Bf 109G, the Spitfire XIV was superior in all departments, including roll rate. Not until late in 1944 did the

Luftwaffe introduce the "long nose" FW 190D, which was roughly its equal, and the jet-powered Messerschmitt Me 262, which was much faster. The first Me 262 to be lost in air combat fell to a Spitfire XIV of No.401 Sqn, on 5 October 1944.

D-DAY

During 1943, the 2nd Tactical Air Force (2TAF) was formed, in good time for the forthcoming Allied invasion of Europe. It included Spitfire squadrons which were at first equipped with the LF.VC, and later with the LF.IX and its Packard/Merlin-engined derivative, the F.XVI. These were to be based in France as soon as temporary landing grounds could be made secure, in order to provide a quick reaction to German activity. But before the Normandy invasion took place, the V 1 threat had to be neutralized. Accordingly, the launch sites were dive-bombed, some by Spitfires carrying 500lb (227kg) bombs on underwing racks.

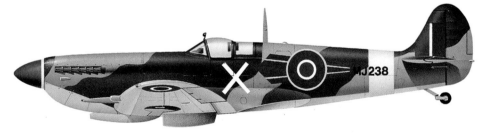

Above: Based at Hal Far airfield on the island of Malta during the latter stages of the war, this No.73 Sqn, RAF, MkIXC is adorned with the distinctive fuselage marking worn by aircraft operated by this unit.

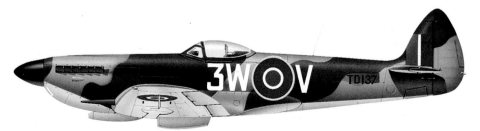

Above: Powered by the US-built Packard Merlin 266, the Spitfire XIVE was used primarily on sorties at low level. Many, including this No.322 Sqn, RAF, example, were fitted with clipped wing tips.

Above: This No.131 Sqn, RAF, MkVIII wears a high-altitude daytime fighter camouflage in connection with its use as a fighter escort for RAF bombers operating against targets in France in late-1944.

Above: Only one front-line RAF unit was equipped with the Spitfire 21 during the Second World War, namely No.91 Sqn, which used the aircraft primarily on armed reconnaissance missions along the Dutch coast.

Above: Post-war RAF operations in the Middle East relied heavily on later models of the Spitfire, such as this FR.XVIII assigned to No.208 Sqn, which could be fitted with a trio of recce cameras.

Above: This PR.XIX, operated by No.81 Sqn, RAF, from Seletar in the early-1950s, was used to photograph vast swathes of jungle as part of RAF anti-guerrilla operations during the protracted Malayan Emergency.

Above: Suitably adorned with black and white D-Day invasion stripes, a No.308 (Polish) Sqn, RAF, MkIX is primed and readied for another fighter-bombing sortie.

Between D-Day on 6 June 1944, and 5 September 1944, Allied fighters flew more than 200,000 sorties, a high proportion of which were undertaken by Spitfires. In reply, the German fighters were able to mount just over 30,000 sorties. This massive imbalance ensured local air superiority over the battle area for the Allies, and nothing German was safe during the hours of daylight, whether in the air or on the gound. A valuable contribution to the Allied war effort was made by Spitfire IXs in the late afternoon of 17 July 1944, when they attacked and strafed General-Feldmarschall Rommel's staff car near Livarot, severely injuring him and putting him out of the war. The Spitfire also made a valuable contribution to RAF morale during this period, when Depth Charge Modification XXX was made to a few Spitfires, enabling them to ferry barrels of beer from England to France on their bomb shackles!

After the war's end, new Spitfire variants continued to come off the production lines, the result of the never-ending quest for better performance. A few of them were destined to see further action, as were a handful of the older models. In the post-war years, RAF Spitfire VIIIs were used against Indonesian

The Missions

Above: A fuel tank is filled with "Joy Juice" (beer) prior to being attached to the Spitfire and flown to British troops in France.

insurgents, while French Spitfire IXs operated against followers of Ho Chi Minh in Indo-China. RAF Spitfire F.XVIIIs and PR.XIXs also flew against the Communist terrorists in Malaya, the last mission taking place on 1 April 1954. The last variant to serve as a front-line fighter with the RAF was the F.24, which served with No.80 Sqn at Hong Kong until January 1952.

The air combat swansong of the Spitfire came in the Middle East, where it clashed with its old opponent, the Me 109, in its Czech-built, Jumo-engined guise as the Avia S199. This came about as the emergent nation of Israel defended itself against its Arab neighbours. The Israelis acquired a handful of S199s with which to counter Egyptian Spitfires; still later they purchased Spitfires from Czechoslovakia, and there were several occasions when these aircraft duelled in the air, pitting Spitfire against Spitfire. The RAF was also involved: on 22 May 1948, Egyptian Spitfire IXs attacked the British air base at Ramat David, probably as a result of faulty intelligence. They were intercepted by Spitfire FR.XVIIIs of No.208 Sqn, RAF, and four were shot down. Another incident occurred on 7 January 1949, when four RAF Spitfire FR.XVIIIs of

No.208 Sqn, now based in Sinai and on an armed reconnaissance sortie, were bounced by two Israeli Spitfire LF.IXs flown by mercenaries. Three of the British fighters were shot down by the Israeli fighters, and the fourth fell to ground fire at much the same time. Later in the day, another surprise attack was made on an RAF formation by four Israeli Spitfires, led by Ezer Weizman. Two RAF Hawker Tempests were lost as a result. Fortunately for the Israelis, only diplomatic measures were taken against them as "punishment" for their actions.

Photo-reconnaissance Spitfires did an invaluable job in all theatres of the war, ranging the length and breadth of occupied Europe and North Africa, as well as Burma, their combination of high-speed and high-altitude flight making them very difficult to intercept. At first rather short-legged, they were later to fly as far as Berlin on pre- and post-strike reconnaissance missions, for which they carried two

Above: Having arrived off Hong Kong aboard an aircraft carrier, this Spitfire F.24 is ferried to the shore aboard a lighter in 1949.

large cameras with 36in (98cm) tele-photo lenses. Normal mission altitudes were between 38,000 and 40,000ft (11,600–12,200m), at a speed of about 350mph (563km/hr). As it would take an interceptor anything up to 30 minutes to reach this altitude, during which time the Spitfire would have travelled some 175 miles (282km), it can be seen that until

Above: Surplus RAF Spitfires, like this LF.IX, found their way into service with the Egyptian Air Force in the post-war years. In time, Egyptian Spitfires would tackle Spitfires flown by Israel.

Above: Assigned to No.101 Sqn of the Israeli Air Force/Defence Force, this F.IXE was the personal mount of Ezer Weizman, the squadron's Commanding Officer and veteran of the Battle of Britain.

Above: Photo-reconnaissance models of the Spitfire played a vital support role on all operational fronts throughout the war.

the jet-powered Me 262 entered service, it was largely a matter of luck whether German fighters could make contact. On extreme-range missions such as those to Berlin, the Spitfire's fuel supply allowed less than half-an-hour over the city, but this was enough for several photographic runs to be made. Among other duties, PR Spitfires kept a close watch on the movements of German capital ships such as the *Bismarck* and the *Tirpitz*.

RECCE TARGETS

Other PR missions were flown at low altitudes using oblique cameras. At low-level, the risk of interception was much greater, and these Spitfires were armed in case they had to fight their way out of trouble. The mission routes were carefully plotted to make such operations unpredictable to the defenders, and also to conceal their objectives. One of the most valuable low-level photographs of the war was taken by Spitfire pilot Tony Hill on 5 December 1941, showing a close-up of the Wurzburg radar at Bruneval – the first event in a sequence leading to a covert airborne raid to snatch the unit on the night of 27 February 1942.

While the Seafire was an excellent fighter once engaged in combat, it was not really suitable for carrierborne operations. The weak main landing gear has already been mentioned, but the Seafire also lacked the endurance for lengthy standing patrols and for long-range escort sorties, both of which are important naval requirements. The recovery of a strike force aboard an aircraft carrier can be a long process, and a fighter short on fuel is always a liability.

The Seafire made its operational debut from the deck of HMS *Furious*, providing much-needed air cover for the Operation "Torch" landings in North Africa in November 1942. Some opposition from Vichy French fighters was encountered, and two Dewoitine D. 520s were shot down. The next major operation was the landings at Salerno, Italy in 1943, for which Seafire IIs provided cover. Fleet Air Arm Seafire IIs and IIIs later operated from shore bases in Italy, and after acting as gunfire "spotters" for British capital ships bombarding the Normandy coast in June 1944, were among the first Allied fighters to be based in France. The Allied landings in the South of France in 1944 were also covered by Seafires. The Seafire III reached the

Pacific theatre early in 1945, from where they flew escort and support missions against oil targets in Sumatra, Japanese-held islands and finally Japan itself. They also provided cover for the seaborne landings at Rangoon and Penang.

The final actions of the Seafire were flown by the Mk47. Operating from HMS *Triumph*, aircraft of No. 800 Squadron, Fleet Air Arm, carried out rocket strikes against Communist terrorist strongholds in Malaya between October 1949 and February 1950. Later that same year, and from the same carrier, No.800 Sqn Seafires flew a total of 360 sorties in the Korean War; 115 of these being ground-attack missions. One Seafire was lost to air action; straying too close to an American bomber, it was mistaken for a Yakovlev Yak-9 by a trigger-happy gunner and shot down.

The last unit of Seafires was retired by the Fleet Air Arm in November 1954, while the last Spitfires in RAF service, the meteorological flight at RAF Woodvale, soldiered on until 1960. Magnificent as the Spitfire/Seafire were, their abilities had been overtaken by technology in the form of the jet engine.

Below: The Supermarine Seafire was to see combat action during the Korean War. This Mk47 is equipped with Rocket-Assisted Take-Off (RATO) units to ease its departure.

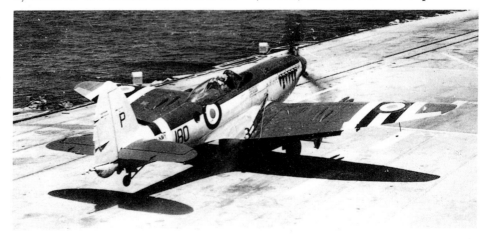

WHILE the Spitfire was designed for a specific defensive function with the RAF, its capabilities were such that even before it had proved itself in combat, many nations were interested in acquiring their own examples. Prior to the outbreak of the Second World War, enquiries and many firm orders had been received from, in alphabetical order: Belgium, Bulgaria, China, Egypt, Estonia, Finland, France, Greece, Holland, Iran, Latvia, Lithuania, Norway, Portugal, Romania, Sweden, Switzerland, Turkey and Yugoslavia. The Japanese, who were evaluating almost everything in sight at this time, asked for one example, while Iceland, for some strange reason, asked for a second-hand Spitfire for instructional purposes! This naturally was not forthcoming. With war imminent, RAF Fighter Command needed all the Spitfires it could get, and most export orders were cancelled, although a single example was delivered to France in July 1939, and two more to Turkey in June 1940.

More than 23,000 Spitfires and Seafires were built in total; the majority of which served with the RAF and the Fleet Air Arm. During early 1940, production was hard pressed to keep pace with attrition, but with the appointment of the dynamic Lord Beaverbrook as Minister of Aircraft Production, stocks began to mount, and the situation, although serious, never really became critical. Pilot shortage, on the other hand, was far graver, and an

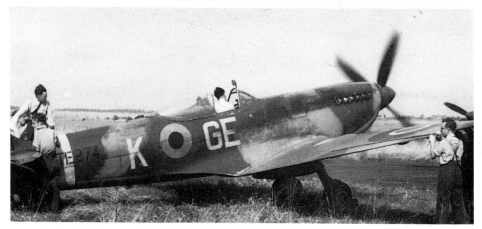

Above: Belgium was one of several European nations to order Spitfires, but it was not until the post-war years that ex-RAF aircraft became widely available for export.

influx of trained pilots from occupied countries was put to good use; national squadrons being formed within Fighter Command. This eventually gave rise to Free French, Polish, Czech, Belgian, Dutch and Norwegian Spitfire squadrons within the RAF, although some of these came considerably later. Commonwealth countries also provided personnel, resulting in Canadian, Australian and New Zealand squadrons being formed. At the end of the war, most were to take their Spitfires home with them, to form the nuclei of their post-war Air Forces.

Above: A Spitfire IIB operated by No.306 (Polish) Squadron, RAF, in August 1941. Note the prominent red and white Polish national insignia located on the fuselage.

Left: A clipped-wing Spitfire VB, one of 40 examples acquired by the Portuguese Air Force in 1947, and in use until the mid-1950s.

Supermarine Spitfire

Above: Turkey was one of over a dozen foreign air arms to operate examples of the MkV. This example is a MkVb, complete with Vokes tropical air filter fairing.

From the outset of war, a stream of American volunteers made their way across the Atlantic to join the fight against Hitler. At first they were just a handful, but, as many of them posed as Canadians,

there were more than is generally thought. The first Eagle squadron, No.71, was formed in October 1940, although it did not become operational for nearly a year. It was followed in May 1941 by No.121 Sqn, and shortly after by No.133 Sqn. When the USA entered the war, two squadrons of the 31st Fighter Group were equipped with Spitfire Vs, as was the 52nd Fighter Group, having traded in its Bell P.39 Airacobras which had suffered badly at the hands of the Luftwaffe. Then, in September 1942, the Eagle trio transferred to the United States Army Air Force (USAAF) to become the 334th, 335th and 336th Fighter Squadrons of the 4th Fighter Group, retaining their Spitfires until the following Spring. A considerable number of PR Spitfires were also used by the USAAF. The US Navy also flew Spitfires, using them to spot for naval gunfire during the Normandy landings.

SOUTHERN SUPPLIES

The Middle Eastern and Italian campaigns also saw Spitfires widely used; when supplies permitted, many South African and Southern Rhodesian Air Force fighter squadrons re-equipped with the type, which was generally used to replace the faithful but war-weary Curtiss P-40 Kittyhawks.

Above: The red, white and blue bands on this LF.IX's rudder and spinner identify it as being operated by an RAF squadron with Norwegian links.

Below: Receiving attention at their rough-field base in Italy during 1944, these Spitfire VCs served with No.352 Sqn, Balkan Air Force.

Above: Wearing desert camouflage, this Spitfire MkVIII served with the 308th Fighter Sqn, 31st Fighter Group, USAAF, in Italy during 1944.

Foreign Service

Above: Forsaking camouflage for a natural metal finish, this PR.XI served with the USAAF's 7th Photo Group in England during 1943–44.

Above: Over 1,000 Spitfire IXs were supplied to the Soviet Union, this example being converted in Leningrad to become a two-seat trainer.

Above: The Royal Australian Air Force (RAAF) made extensive use of several Spitfire variants during the war, including the MkVIII.

Above: The orange centre within the fuselage roundel on this MkIX identifies it as an example supplied to the South African Air Force.

SOVIET SERVICE

By 1942, Spitfire production was in full swing, and supplies of aircraft to fronts on which the RAF was not operating became possible. The most important of these recipients was the Soviet Union, which was desperate for any material with which to prosecute the war. Attrition on the Eastern Front was so severe that the average life of a fighter was only about 80 hours. Supply was generally via the notorious PQ convoys to Murmansk, and losses *en route* were high. Supplies of Spitfires to the Soviets began in 1942, and by the time that the battle for the Kuban Bridgehead began in April 1943, several fighter regiments were operational with the type. In all, 4,283 British-built fighters were despatched to the Soviet Union, including 143 Spitfire VBs and 1,188 Spitfire IXs, most of which arrived safely. How the British fighter stood up to the rigours of the Russian winter is not recorded, but towards the end of 1944, a Spitfire in Soviet service was credited with shooting down four German fighters in a single mission.

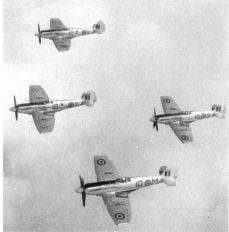

Above: No less than 133 Spitfire XIVs were supplied from RAF stocks to the Belgian Air Force. This quartet comprises two F.XIVs and two camera-equipped FR.XIVs.

Supermarine Spitfire

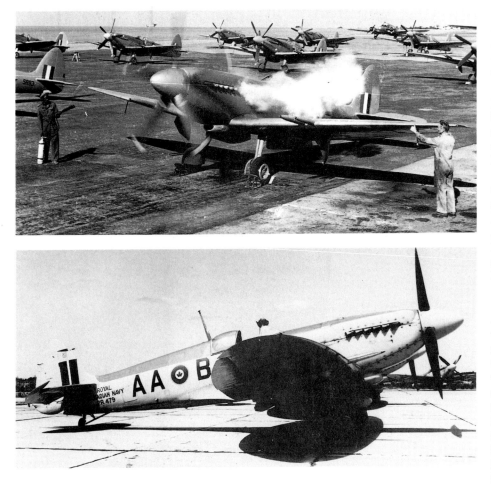

Left: Activity on the flightline at Salisbury airport as a No.1 Squadron Southern Rhodesian Air Force F.22 comes to life with the help of a Coffman cartridge starter.

training tasks. No.8 Sqn, equipped with Spitfire VIIIs, was to be the only Indian squadron to see action during the war, culminating in an attack on a Japanese headquarters at Paingkyon on 11 August 1945. Other Royal Indian Air Force squadrons converted to the Spitfire, including No.6, which operated the MkXIVE, but too late to see combat. After partition in 1947, both Spitfire XVIIIs and PR.XIXs entered front-line service, the former variant remaining in Indian service until 1957.

At the end of the Second World War in 1945, surplus military aircraft abounded. As a result of this, the Spitfire found its way into the service of many nations, notably Israel, most of whose Spitfires were bought from Czechoslovakia. These were used extensively in a shooting war against Israel's Arab neighbours, most of the survivors eventually being sold to Burma. Other countries whose military insignia adorned the Spitfire included: Denmark; Egypt, who used them against Israeli Spitfires; Eire; Greece; Portugal; Syria, who acquired several F.22s from Southern Rhodesia; Thailand; and Yugoslavia. Spitfires also served with the Netherlands East Indies Air Force, the Czech Air Police and the French Aeronavale.

Above: A Seafire F.XV as operated by No.883 Sqn, Royal Canadian Navy, at Dartmouth, Nova Scotia.

The Spitfire was also used as a political pawn during the Second World War. In the Eastern Mediterranean, it was essential to keep Turkey at least neutral. After Germany had supplied Turkey with some FW 190s, it became expedient to provide Spitfires to even up the balance. A trade-off was also attempted with Sweden: Spitfires would be supplied with the proviso that Swedish ball bearings would not be supplied to Germany, but in this case the ploy failed, and Sweden had to wait until after hostilities ceased before getting the fighters she wanted.

The Royal Indian Air Force received Spitfires in time to use them in action against the Japanese. Initially, a handful of Spitfire VCs was delivered in October 1944, these being used for pilot conversion

Above: An ex-Czechoslovak Air Force Spitfire IXE in the markings of the fledgling Israeli Defence Force/ Air Force, during the early-1950s.

INDEX